The Humble Idealist

A handbook to *Healing of a Wounded Idealist*

The Humble Idealist

Cover: Jabulile Mkonza
http://vision-imc.com

To all idealists, everywhere.
Bold, visionary,
and easily wounded.

Contents

The Humble Idealist

*It was pride that changed angels
into devils; it is humility
that makes men as angels.*
Augustine

In *Healing of a Wounded Idealist,* we asserted that if you scratch under the surface of a cynic you will find a wounded idealist. A person, who despite their sceptical and at times, brazen exterior, is actually deeply disappointed. Life and relationships have not turned out how they had expected, and their youthful hopes and dreams for the future are tainted. Spiritual life is equally disillusioning. From initial zeal and optimism, it is reduced to the struggle of keeping long-held convictions alive. Yet, as we discovered, there is hope! It is not an unfamiliar place for *many* biblical heroes.

Disclaimer

But before we get ahead of ourselves, we need to make a disclaimer. In *Healing of a Wounded Idealist,* we put forward that an idealist should aim at becoming what we phrased a "faithful realist." After further consideration, we have recognised that an idealist will fundamentally remain an idealist, and it would be unrealistic to think of changing the nature that God gave us at birth. However, the way for an idealist to avoid the trap of cynicism remains the same: humility.

And this brings us to the reason for writing, *The Humble Idealist*.

We never planned to write a second book, but after receiving a lot of feedback on the link between a cynic, a wounded idealist, and humility, the need for further discussion became evident. "How does one *practically* navigate the waters of cynicism to faith?" How can idealism become faith?

Our Proposal

What we propose, is that if cynics or wounded idealists are to find the path to faith, they must retrace the steps that led to cynicism. They must gain greater awareness, and recognise the choices made, and the steps taken, that damaged their faith. If we follow the path to wounding it may look something like this:

> First, an idealist is disappointed, then discouraged, then disillusioned, then angered, and finally becomes cynical. Each step could take months or years to make.

To find faith, we must backtrack through each step, using humility as a guide.

On a note: We have written this handbook in such a way that it can be read from front to back or back to front, or just the chapters that apply. Our only encouragement is that you would *take your time*. Read the scriptures, answer the questions, consider the points.

Is this as Good as it Gets?

If you are a cynic or are still battling to overcome cynicism, we hear you! People have let you down, and you feel that God has done the same. You fundamentally believe that it will happen again. You are suspicious of people's motives and intentions. There are few people you trust, and fewer you respect. You smirk at others' lofty ambitions and ideals, ideals you may once have held. You *now* know better; disappointment has enlightened your soul. But beware. T. S. Eliot wrote:

Disillusion can become an illusion if we rest in it.[1]

While having a cynical outlook may keep most people at a safe distance, it can be a lonely place to live. It will isolate you from the life that God has planned for you; that is still planned for you. You may have given up on your spiritual dreams but God has not given up on you. This is *not* as good as it gets. There is another road to take.

Why It Matters

Interestingly, the potential for cynicism is not specific to the church. You will find it in all organisations that attract idealists and hold out an agenda for change in society. Politics and activism are clear examples. In his book, *The Long Game: A Memoir,* US Senator Mitch McConnell describes the zeal with which new interns embrace positions in Washington. He even refers to them as humble idealists, but describes their "selfless

---

[1]T.S. Eliot.The Complete Poems and Plays of T. S. Eliot.(2011) Faber

pursuit of justice and truth" as largely a fable.*2*

In *Confessions of a Greenpeace Dropout,* Dr. Patrick Moore, a co-founder, and leader in the Green Peace Movement chronicles his involvement and eventual disillusionment with the organisation.*3* Even in South Africa, to the dismay of many anti-apartheid activists, the concept of a post-apartheid Rainbow Nation*4* championed by Nelson Mandela, is considered "a distant and rapidly disappearing dream."*5*

These are just a few examples of cynicism in society at large, but for Christians, the stakes are too high to just accept cynicism in our churches. It literally is a matter of eternal life or death.

Into the mind of a Christian Cynic

Cynics, like idealists, consider themselves to be unique. The Bible says that *no temptation has seized us except what is common to man.*6 This is of little consequence to a cynic. They believe that how they feel, and what they think is unique. The problem with feeling unique is that you believe that nobody can relate, no one understands, and therefore no one can help.

---

2 McConnell, Mitch. The Long Game: A Memoir. (2016) Sentinel

3 Moore, P. Confessions of a green peace dropout 2010 Beatty St Publishing

4 A term coined by Archbishop Tutu describing the unity of people from different ethnic groups, in a country once divided by black and white.

5 www.news24.com/Columnists/GuestColumn/let-us-revisit-the-idea-of-a-rainbow-nation-20180323

6 1 Corinthians 10:13

Be that as it may, consider the perspective of a Christian cynic:

"When I make it to church, I sit near the back. Regularly
missing church no longer bothers me, in fact, it's a relief to not
have to put up a front and be with people I don't really like. If I
am this unhappy, why do I still come to church? Maybe it's
part ritual, maybe it's punching in my card to appease my
conscience and hopefully do enough to make it to heaven.
Because ultimately God knows my heart. He knows that I love
him, I just don't want to be involved with the people, the
commitments, and all the expectations. He knows my heart.
That is comforting. Or wait, is it? He knows my heart...
He knows how I have been hurt, he also knows my lack of
willingness to forgive or even to express my hurts. He has seen
my anger. Nothing changes, it all stays the same. He knows my
disappointment with *Him*. Again and again, I prayed. I even
begged, but what has happened, happened. The Lord's will be
done. Honestly, what's the point of praying when God is going
to do what he wants to anyway... but let me not go there. I
would rather make it about other things than being
disappointed or let down or feeling useless and ineffective.
How pathetic does that sound?! So now I sit at the back. I still
have passion, but it's for things that give me a sense of
significance outside of the church institution. That's right,
institution. I once considered it a family, a home, a safe place
away from the chaos of the world, but now I see it for what it
is; another organisation with flawed leaders and imperfect
followers. Why do I keep coming? People are so naive. The
other day I heard a young preacher speak about faith. Let's give
that man some time! He can come and talk to me when he's
been around a while, then let's see how faithful he is..."

We could go on. Relate to some of it, a bit of it, all of it?

Moving Forward by Stepping Back

Thankfully it doesn't have to end here. In their book, *The 10 Laws of Boundaries*, psychologists Cloud and Townsend, describe a reactive phase where a person recognises and rejects a state of powerlessness which may have developed from his or her own or others' expectations, and/or manipulation. But they ask an important question on the road to self-empowerment.

> "But when is enough, enough? Reaction phases are necessary but not sufficient for the establishment of boundaries. It is crucial for the two-year-old to throw the peas at Mommy, but to continue that until forty-three is too much. A reactive stage is a stage, not an identity. Do not stay there. Spiritual adulthood has higher goals than "finding yourself." Proactive people are very different from those who are known by what they hate, what they don't like, or what they stand against, and will not do. Emotionally, the reactive stance brings diminishing returns. You must react to find your own boundaries, but having found them, you must not "use your freedom to satisfy your sinful nature." Galatians 5:13 Eventually, you must rejoin the human race you have reacted to, and establish connections as equals, loving your neighbour as yourself."[7]

If a Christian idealist has formed unhelpful spiritual patterns and ways of interacting with a disappointing world, they need to become aware of these reactions and learn new paths towards faith and spiritual maturity, instead of following the well-worn path that leads to cynicism. It's time to go back to move forward.

---

[7] Dr. Cloud & Dr. Townsend.10 Laws of Boundaries, 2017. Zondervan

Moses

No one can go back and make a
brand new start, but anyone can start
now and have a brand new end.

One can only imagine the brooding thoughts Moses was entertaining as he sat in the Midian desert trying to make sense of what had happened to the wondrous life he had had in Egypt. It had fallen apart so quickly, almost overnight. It started when he tried to save a Hebrew slave from his Egyptian master. He had been waiting for a chance to reveal himself as one of Israel's deliverers when the opportunity presented itself. He had imagined the gratitude and awe the Hebrews would feel knowing that they had one of their own in the palace, working on their behalf. But instead of the praise and recognition he expected, he received scorn and rejection from the people he was trying to help. They weren't appreciative of his heroic meddling and questioned his motives.[8]

The book of Acts gives us deeper insight into what he was thinking:

> "Moses thought that his own people would realise that God was using him to rescue them, **but they did not**."[9]

The lack of recognition (and a death threat from Pharaoh), was

---

[8] Exodus 2:11-15

[9] Acts 7:24-33

enough to cause him to abandon his brave facade and run from the life, culture, and country he had always known. (Deeply disappointed idealists run away, or are at least tempted to. We wonder how many disillusioned idealists have ended, or almost ended, a marriage or a relationship, quit a job, or left the church, because the hurt of unmet expectations was more than they felt they could bear. They aren't cowards as some may think; they are reeling from the pain of being unable to reconcile their reality with their idealistic expectations.)

So at the age of forty, Moses left Egypt; a wounded man. He made a new life for himself in a literal and figurative desert and would stay away from friends and family for another forty years. He named his firstborn son, Gershom,[10] a reminder that he was now a foreigner. A man without a home or national identity.

If God had left Moses there, his story would have faded into obscurity. Perhaps remembered in Egyptian folklore as a tale about, *a baby drawn from the water, given by the gods to become a prince of Egypt, and mysteriously returned to the gods*. But this was not where his story ended.

God Found Him

When God engaged Moses in the desert, he knew it would not be a simple re-introduction. Moses had let go of the path he had imagined his life would take as a young idealist. He had licked his wounds, picked himself up, and was now on a different road. A road that no longer ended in him serving the

---

[10] Exodus 2:22 Gershom meaning foreigner

God of the Israelites. But God, in his infinite wisdom, knows how to reach us, even in the deepest pit, or furthest desert. And although it took Moses a while to work through his doubts and excuses; he did, and became one of the most influential religious leaders in human history.[11] Despite how it may have seemed, Moses had never been beyond God's reach.

And so, at the age of eighty, Moses returned to Egypt; a changed man. The book of Acts describes his return like this:

> "God sent back the *same man* his people had previously rejected when they demanded, 'Who made you a ruler and judge over us?' God sent Moses to be their ruler and deliverer."[12]

God didn't find someone new to rescue his people. There was no plan B. God's plan always involved Moses. He had given Moses opportunities, both successes and defeats, to train him for his purpose. God would wait for him to overcome what he needed to, and to heal. And once Moses was ready, God sent back the *same man*. And through God's power, he did wonders in Egypt. We know the stories; the plagues, the negotiations, the back and forth, until finally Pharaoh let the people go. And when they did, Moses got a *second chance* to leave Egypt. But this time Moses did not flee. This time he left in faith and not in fear.[13] This time he left seeing him who is invisible and was

---

[11] All three monotheistic world religions claim Moses as their own. Judaism and Christianity make obvious claims, but even in Islam, Moses is mentioned more often in the Q'ran than any other individual, including Abraham and Mohammad.

[12] Acts 7:35 NLT

[13] Exodus 7-11

not blinded by his own wounding.[14]

It really is an astounding story. But how was it possible? We have proposed that humility is the way back to faith when we have been wounded. So how do we see it played out in Moses' life?

The younger Moses was anything but humble. In their initial meeting in the desert, Moses refused God six times before agreeing to do what God asked. Twice he debated with God on the rationale behind the action plan, and he regularly expressed his frustration to God and with God.[15] Even the conversations and questions we are privy to show a man with strong opinions and entitlement issues; hardly an example of a meek and self-effacing spirit.

"Why, Lord, why have you brought trouble on this people?" Exodus 5:22

"You have not rescued your people at all." Exodus 5:23

"Now show me your glory." Exodus 33:18

"If this is how you are going to treat me, please go ahead and kill me." Numbers 11:15

Yet a later character reference reveals a very different man.

In Numbers 12:3 it reads:

Now Moses was a very humble man, more humble than

---

[14] Hebrews 11:27

[15] See Exodus 32:11-13, Numbers 14:11-16

16

anyone else on the face of the earth.

So how do we reconcile his later reputation with what we see in his earlier character? And more importantly, why does it matter for idealists who have been wounded? Since this astonishing description of the older Moses is in line with our premise of the need for humility, we will investigate it further.

> From the outset, the distinction needs to be made between being **humbled** and being **humble**. The Bible doesn't say that Moses was the most humbled man on the face of the earth.[16] To be sure, God humbled Moses. Raised as a Prince of Egypt, he went from walking the halls of Pharaoh's palace to tending flocks as a shepherd, an occupation the Egyptians detested.[17] He *was* humbled, but by allowing God to work in and through him, in time, he became a humble man — but perhaps not in the traditional sense of the word.

Hallowed Be My Name

To understand the enormity of the statement made of him later in life, we need to understand the culture in which Moses was raised. The Egyptians were a proud race. The Pharaohs were considered an incarnation of the gods and society was set up to worship them. They were obsessed with grand titles and their eternal legacy. Jewish writer, S. H. Parker notes that the Pharaohs were so determined to be glorified, they rarely gave any credit to their predecessors. For example, Ramses II

---

[16] Perhaps Job fits that category best

[17] Genesis 36:41-16.

eradicated, literally erased, his father's name from every building his father had constructed, and wrote his own name over it.[18]

Being a part of Pharaoh's household meant that you were better than everybody else, and enjoyed the best of everything, from education to the latest medical advances. The reverence and adoration of the royals was so ingrained in the culture, one would hardly have blamed the young Moses if he thought he was the god's gift to mankind!

My Kingdom Come

When God gave Moses the extraordinary trust and responsibility of leading his people, it would not have been a stretch for him to default to the worldly way of thinking he had been brought up with: "I am God's gift to these people, they are lucky to have me." Maybe he could have given himself a new title, *Grand Super Leader*, or set up a statue or monument in his honour. (King Saul did it in 1 Samuel 15.) He could have appointed bodyguards and representatives to establish his importance and keep the commoners at a distance. Perhaps commission the dressmakers to make a multicoloured coat with matching headpiece. The possibilities were endless!

And yet we see none of this.

Even in death, Moses was markedly different from the culture that raised him. While the Pharaohs spent lifetimes building magnificent tombs and pyramids to be buried in and eternally

---

[18] www.par2.com/humble.htm

remembered, Moses died and was buried in an unmarked grave. *Take a moment and let that sink in.*

In understated commentary the Bible offers two verses to the event:

And Moses the servant of the Lord died there in Moab, as the Lord had said. He buried him in Moab, in the valley opposite Beth Peor, *but to this day no one knows where his grave is.*[19]

To this day no one knows where this great man is buried! Unlike his Egyptian ancestors, he had made no preparations for his death and burial. There would be no shrine, no tomb, no pilgrimage, no honour, and no exaltation.

Hallowed Be Your Name

Robert Ingersoll said:

> Most people can bear adversity. But if you wish to know what a man really is, give him power.[20]

In this sense, Moses set a sterling example of humility. S. H. Parker offers a deeper understanding of the humility that Moses displayed before God.

"As often as Moses resisted God's will by saying no, as many uprisings as he put down, and judgments he rendered, there was one thing he never did. He never took credit that was not rightfully his. He always gave credit to God, for God's actions.

---

[19] Deuteronomy 34:5-6

[20] Robert G. Ingersoll, The Works of Robert G. Ingersoll, Vol. 3 (of 12) Dresden Edition-Lectures

He never once claimed to have led Israel out of Egypt or to have freed them or given them the law. When his authority was challenged, he never lashed out, "Do you know who I am!?" No, rather Moses prostrated himself and let God work it out. He did not jealously guard his authority. He knew who had given it and who could take it away."[21]

Moses' humility gave him the ability to recognise his rightful place before God. He was not God or even a god, but God's servant. He wasn't looking for acknowledgment, credit, or praise. It was not his concern nor his business. It wasn't about him and it never would be. God had found him in a dark, disappointed place and given him a second chance. The Bulgarian poet, Katerina Stoykova Klemer, wrote:

> "If pain doesn't lead to humility, you have wasted your suffering." [22]

Moses did not waste his suffering. Granted, God had to coax him out of the desert and re-ignite his heart, but he got up again! He made that choice. The wounds did not define his end.

Your Will be Done

The question is, are we willing to do the same? If you have become cynical, God has not given up on you. Even now he is coaxing you out of the desert you have created for yourself. You are not beyond his reach. Will you humble yourself and allow him to re-ignite your soul? Before you answer that, maybe we should clarify what we mean. The humility we see

---

[21] www.par2.com/humble.htm

[22] K. Stoykova Klemer. The Porcupine of Mind. 2012. Broadstone Books

displayed in Moses' life does not mean keeping quiet or having no opinions or emotions. In fact, it may mean having a greater voice, stronger opinions and an abundance of emotions. But their source and goal are different.

Moses was wounded and got back up again, but even as he lived out God's will for his life, he still battled with anger, disappointment, disillusionment and discouragement. He remained an idealist, after all, just one determined to be humble before God. Moses' life teaches us a deeper sense of humility and it shows us that regardless of our starting point, humility can grow over time; each time we choose to trust and submit to God.

Over the next chapters we will follow Moses' life, his example and his journey in embracing humility.

The Angry Idealist

For a wounded idealist, unrelenting low-grade anger is the final step before turning over to cynicism. Cynics don't have the energy for anger. They have resigned themselves to acceptance by disengagement. So in a sense, the upside of feeling angry if you are a wounded idealist, is that you are still in the fight. You may be fighting the wrong battles, but you are still in it!

In his book, *Anger is a Choice*, Tim LaHaye describes **righteous anger** as:

> a godly indignation towards sin, and is *never* in response to personal rejection, insult or injury.[23]

This is not the kind of anger we are describing here. The anger we are talking about is a result of *having had enough.* Enough of being let down, and enough of feeling disappointed. And it is very personal!

Righteous Anger Defined

LaHaye goes on to list the differences between righteous and unrighteous anger; given in the following chart:

---

[23] T. LaHaye, Anger is a Choice. Zondervan. 2002

Righteous Anger	Unrighteous Anger
Controlled, with purpose	Uncontrolled, without patience
No hatred, malice or resentment	Fuelled with hatred, malice or resentment
Unselfish	Selfish
An expression of concern and care	An expression of personal offense
Aimed to correct or curtail destructive behaviour	Aimed to destroy or hurt the individual
Aimed at injustice or wilful disobedience	Aimed at violations of self or people who oppose you

There is a time and a place when anger is a righteous response,[24] but for our purposes, we want to focus on the anger that hurts us emotionally, physically and more importantly, spiritually. And so we turn once again to Moses.

Moses and Aaron gathered the assembly in front of the rock and said to them, "Listen, you rebels, must we bring you water out of this rock?" Then Moses raised his arm and struck the rock twice with his staff. Water gushed out, and the community and their livestock drank. But the Lord said to Moses and Aaron, "Because you did not trust in me enough to honor me as holy in the sight of the Israelites, you will not bring this community into the land I give them." Numbers 20:10-11

The Israelite community had gathered in opposition to Moses

---

[24] Ephesians 4:26 says, "In your anger do not sin." Anger itself is not a sin, but can lead us to sin. We see many Biblical examples of godly people, and God himself, filled with righteous anger.

and Aaron. This time it was about a lack of water. Exasperated, Moses takes their complaint to God, who tells him to *speak* to the rock. In anger and frustration, Moses *hits* the rock.[25]

Not What I Expected

We can't be sure why Moses reacted this way; it wasn't the first time the Israelites had complained. He had faithfully endured their grumbling for years, why was this time so different? It could have just been the proverbial straw that broke the camel's back, but we think that it may have been something a lot more personal.

In Numbers 20:1, a verse before the water saga began, the Bible tells us that Miriam, Moses' sister, had died and been buried. Miriam had been a tremendous support to Moses, from the days when she watched over his small basket in the reeds, to helping him watch over Israel.[26] She was his big sister and friend, and now… she was gone. Perhaps the emotional strain and grief were more than Moses felt he could bear, and maybe, he had *expected* the people to be understanding and give him a little time and space. Maybe take their demands to someone else, and allow him a moment to grieve and focus on his own needs. But they hadn't! And he had had enough.

Expectations

An angry idealist has had one too many unmet expectations. If he or she were to have a personal mantra, it would go

---

[25] Numbers 20:2-12

[26] Exodus 15:20-21

something like this:

> It is not right. It is not fair.
> It should not be this way.
> It should be different.

They have had expectations, "reasonable expectations" of people and God, but have learned that people are not dependable, and God is unpredictable. They no longer live hopeful of what life could be. They insist on how it should be. And it angers them that it isn't.

Expectations are tricky. They disguise themselves as goals, visions, hopes, assumptions and social norms. Every time, you think someone **should** do something or something **should** happen, that is an expectation.[27] For Christians, they can mask themselves as faith, and when unmet, they can cause havoc in our spiritual lives.

> We know of a couple, where the wife was diagnosed with a very aggressive form of skin cancer and was given two months to live. The family was obviously devastated. The husband, in a misguided sense of faith, resolved that God would answer his prayers to completely heal his wife. He would not allow anyone, including his wife, to be "faithless" or in any way negative. People were not permitted to cry when visiting their home, or talk of any outcome other than a miraculous healing. The wife's condition declined rapidly. Because of her husband's decision, she was never given the opportunity to write letters to their

---

[27] www.nerdycreator.com/blog/no-expectations-no-disappointment/

three young children; a treasure for their futures, as that would have been faithless. Within a couple of months, she died. In anger, the husband turned away from God. He had expected God to heal his wife, and God had not.

This is a very sad story but is a stark example of how we can confuse expectations with faith. Whereas faith is actively trusting God, and leaving the outcome and our happiness in his hands, expectations are just mental creations. They are projections of the mind into what the future should be, or of what God or others should do/be for us. Albert Einstein made an interesting observation of the potential pitfall of expectations in marriage when he noted:

> Men marry women with the hope they will never change.
> Women marry men with the hope that they will change.
> Invariably both are disappointed.[28]

Acceptance

The opposite of expectations is acceptance. While expectations are based in the imaginary, acceptance is grounded in reality. Regardless of what an idealist imagines — we cannot be truly happy until we accept life on life's terms. Or as Charlie Brown would say:

> The best thing one can do when it's raining,
> is to let it rain.

The truth is that life isn't fair. The story doesn't always have a

---

[28] Albert Einstein, Quotes (1879-1955)

happy ending. Good things happen to bad people and bad things happen to good people. Many times justice, and what is right, *do not* prevail. People (even Christians), are inherently selfish and prideful. Society worships the strong and tramples the weak. Things are not how we hope they would be, and it's not about to change anytime soon. Author Stewart O'nan noted:

> You have to accept your life as a whole.
> You couldn't relive your life and skip the awful bits,
> without losing what made it worthwhile.

There is an irony in acceptance. It is not a passive defeat, but a source of freedom. If we look back at Moses' anger towards the Israelites; how differently would things have turned out if he had just accepted them for who they were? He had led them in the desert for years. They were stubborn, difficult, unruly and demanding. He knew this about them. Why did he expect them to be any different because he had a need? It was not reality, but a mental projection. If he had accepted them, and not been so personally offended, he would have *spoken* to the rock, and then two amazing things would have happened. Firstly, the Israelites would have received their water, and secondly, Moses would have had the time he needed to grieve and find his strength in God. (Not to mention the fact that he would have been able to enter the Promised Land!)

So how can an angry idealist find some peace and acceptance, and choose a path that leads to faith rather than taking the next step towards cynicism?

THE BRIDGE OF HUMILITY

Step One: **Let go of expectations, but express your needs.**

Letting go of expectations doesn't mean that we allow people to treat us however they want to, without us being able to say something. The key is to make our expectations or mental projections *real*, by expressing them. For example lets say that you have the following expectations of the people around you:

- My friends *should* be more considerate.
- My boss *should* be more understanding.
- My spouse *should* take out the trash.
- My colleagues *should* be more helpful.

And these expectations go unmet.

In most cases, the real reason we are disappointed is not that our spouse didn't take out the trash, or our boss wasn't more understanding or our colleagues weren't more helpful or our friends more considerate. We are disappointed because we expect people to do or be these things without us having to ask. Maybe we feel like that's what *we would do*, or at least, that's what decent people should do.[29]

> This is where we need to apply acceptance and be reminded that at times, we also let people down. There are things people expect of us that we cannot or do not do. We want (even demand), mercy in those areas. Rather than judging those around us, we should show

---

[29] www.nerdycreator.com/blog/no-expectations-no-disappointment/

them the same mercy we would like to be shown.[30]

Rather than hoping that people will anticipate your needs, say something. Even the people closest to you cannot read your mind and it's unfair to expect that of them. Tell them your needs, express your hurts, communicate.

Step Two: Identify Who or What you Blame

When we have unmet or unspoken expectations, we can more easily assign blame. When Moses recounts the story of "rockgate,"[31] he tells the Israelites that *they* were the reason he was excluded from the promised land. They should not have been so difficult to lead.

> "It was because of you the Lord was angry
> with me and would not listen to me."[32]

Moses struck the rock in anger and pointed his finger at the Israelites. In our anger, we can do the same thing; react to something that happens to us and then point a finger.

Who or what do you blame?

- What should be different in your life?
- Who should have treated you differently, or done something

---

[30] The Biblical standard for acceptance is a high calling: Accept one another, then, *just as Christ accepted you.* Romans 15:7

[31] Watergate (a political scandal involving President Nixon in 1972), and its derivatives have been used in media to connote misconduct.

[32] Deuteronomy 3:26

for you?

- What should God have done for you or made clear to you?
- Who or what has let you down?
- What have you had to endure or suffer through, that you cannot find an explanation or meaning for?
- What do you feel is not right or fair?

There is a temptation when you have experienced the pain of life to ask God, "Why me?" And without being conscious of doing it, we can justify our question by giving God our credentials. "I am a good person, I have prayed, I have fasted, I have pleaded. I have tried my best." We can take it a step further by comparing ourselves to people who we perceive as less good. "I am not like that sinner… Why have they been blessed or spared? It's not fair." John Piper offers an illustrative description of the two sides of the pride coin:

Boasting is the response of pride to success.
Self-pity is the response of pride to suffering.[33]

We may not say it out loud, but after accounting for our own goodness, we reach the clear and obvious conclusion: We should not have to suffer, and God should see that. And without humility to steady us, our faith takes a beating.

Suggestion: Ask yourself who you blame and what you feel is unfair. Then look at what you need to take responsibility for. Go beyond the anger and the "power" you feel it may give you. Find true empowerment by facing yourself, and by owning your life and reactions.

---

[33] John Piper, Future Grace. Multnomah Books. 2005

Step Three: Find That Day

Once you have recognised your expectations, and who you blame, you can set your spiritual GPS to HOME.

> "Do not harden your hearts as you did at Meribah,
> as you did *that day* at Massah in the wilderness,
> where your ancestors tested me; they tried me,
> though they had seen what I did.
> Psalm 95:8

During the 40 years the Israelites wandered in the desert, despite their complaining and grumbling, their hearts remained relatively soft. Maybe "soft" is too generous, let's call it childish. However, in Psalm 95, God pinpoints an exact day when that was no longer the case. The day when they deliberately decided to harden their hearts. He knew the day, the place and the decision.

He knows *your* day, too. Do you?

At times, we all feel angry, hurt, upset, irritated, bugged and fed up. Usually, we get over it by taking a nap, eating some food, speaking to a friend, or praying. Depending on how far we have taken our frustrations, we may need to ask for forgiveness and repent. These are the normal struggles we all face as we walk the Christian life.

But then there's that one day.

That Day

The day when we feel, "I just don't care anymore. I don't care about the way I am behaving or the things that I am thinking." On that day, we decide that following God may not be worth it and that we will take life into our own hands. We still come to church, and the fellowship, and even read and pray, but there is a part of our hearts that has hardened, and a new path has been forged. That Day may not be a big event, in fact, it's more of a decision; made days, months or even years before we finally act out.

When we counsel people who have gotten themselves stuck spiritually, we encourage them to find That Day. It's amazing how quickly and clearly they are able to pinpoint it. The decision they made, in the car, on a Thursday. The day they decided not to care anymore and to no longer guard their hearts.

You may ask, why is it so important to find that day? Maybe an illustration will be helpful.

Making it Real

> Let's say that your day was three years ago. The day you decided to return a text message to a person you knew was deliberately flirting with you. Maybe you had been fending off their advances for a while, then something happened at work or home, and you felt let down by people or God, and so, on That Day, sitting in your car or on the bus, you decided to return the text. (Just a note: it wouldn't be That Day if, after sending the text you realised what you were doing and got open about it, and cut off ties with the flirtatious person. We all make rash decisions and do and say dumb things we

regret later, but this is different.)

You send the text and decide that it doesn't matter. You decide to keep it hidden and let the chips fall where they may. From That Day on, many other decisions are made, the consequences of which may only become evident much later. Decisions to be deceitful, to harbour bitterness, to be lazy, to become increasingly selfish and not to care about anyone. It may lead to swearing, smoking, impurity/immorality and drinking... but be sure of this, it all started on That Day. You must find That Day if you have any hope of returning to the path that leads to faith.

Let's fast forward three years. Since That Day, you have gotten yourself into a whole lot of sin. You have hurt many relationships. You now start to lose your faith and long-held beliefs.

(On another note: When we start losing belief in the truth of the Bible, God, and true doctrine, the Bible says it is because we are in sin. Read Hebrews 3:12)

In a moment of spiritual awakening, you decide that this cannot continue. But when you try to make sense of what's happened in your life, it's a mess, and you can't make heads or tails of it. You have spent the last three years justifying yourself and blaming God and others, and now you don't know how to come unstuck.

Find That Day. When you do, you can start taking responsibility for the decisions you have made, and face up to the consequences of those decisions.

Step 4: Run Through the Door

No temptation has overtaken you except what is common to
mankind. And God is faithful; he will not let you be tempted
beyond what you can bear. But when you are tempted, he will
also provide a way out so that you can endure it.[34]

Angry idealist, God is with you. He has not forsaken you. He
has been there the whole time, even as you have wandered
down a different path. He has ensured that you have not been
tempted beyond what you can bear, and that you have always
had a choice. He has constantly provided ways out and
opportunities for you to get help. He has been faithful, even in
your most faithless moment. Even now he is providing a way
out. Get open with a trusted friend about That Day, and
everything else that has happened since. Don't let your anger
shut the door on God's provision. Take the opportunity before
it is too late.

Anger is a trap that will slowly suffocate your spiritual heart,
(and your physical heart).[35] Life and people can be extremely
disappointing, but humility empowers us to acknowledge our
hurts and fears, and not run or distract from them. The path to
your healing lies before you. Humility awaits your response.

---

[34] 1 Corinthians10:13

[35] www.webmd.com/heart-disease/features/rein-in-rage-anger-heart-
disease#1

Self-Awareness

Wisdom tends to grow in proportion
to one's awareness of one's ignorance.
Anthony de Mello

Self-awareness is essential for personal and spiritual growth. The book of Proverbs says:

> The purposes of a person's heart are deep waters,
> but one who has insight draws them out.[36]

The longer we live, the more we realise just how deep those waters run. We all need insight to understand our own hearts! When we get to know ourselves better; our personalities, our strengths, weaknesses, and motivations, we are able to understand why we respond the way we do in different situations. We are able to take responsibility for what we can control, and accept the areas we can't. There is a fundamental truth about life that goes like this:

> We don't see things as they are,
> we see them as WE are.[37]

Despite what we believe to be real, we all filter life through our own subjective belief systems and experiences. As we become more self-aware, we are able to recognise these filters and adjust our perspective.

---

[36] Proverbs 20:5

[37] Although attributed to many writers, its actual origin is unclear

Four Helpful Questions in becoming more Self-Aware

1. What energises you? Spending time with people or spending time alone? Are you an introvert or extrovert? (You can be a loud introvert or a quiet extrovert — the defining distinction is what energises you.)
2. What makes you feel loved? The 5 Love Languages,[38] is an excellent book that addresses this. The key areas are: Quality time, gifts, acts of service, physical touch and words of affirmation.
3. What temperament do you have? There are 4 basic types: sanguine, choleric, melancholic, and phlegmatic. (They can overlap.) A great definition of the basic differences is: A sanguine wants to do something the fun way, cholerics want it done *their* way, a phlegmatic wants to do it the easy way, and a melancholic wants to do it the right way.
4. Are you more naturally accused or deceived in the way you view yourself, and the consequences of your actions? (For more on this, see the chapter on the guilt-ridden idealist in the appendix.)

These are a few simple questions you should be able to answer about yourself. There are great books (and online articles/quizzes) that can further explain each question, and how they affect your outlook and relationships.[39]

---

[38] The Five Love Languages. Gary Chapman. Northfield Publishing. 1992.

[39] For a more in-depth study in understanding how your past influences your present we recommend, *I Choose Us,* and *Good Enough Parenting,* by John and Karen Louis. Publishers: Louis Counselling & Training Services. 2010

One More Question

We want to add another, less obvious, question that will be helpful for you to be able to answer.

    5.   What is your core fear?

Have you ever wondered why some interactions with people really bother you and others not? Knowing your core fear will help you to understand why. Irene and I have been in ministry for over 25 years, but neither of us were aware of what our core fears were, or how we would react when they are triggered. We found the Core Fears Test in the book, *The DNA of Relationships,*[40] by Gary Smalley, and it has been life changing! We have used it in our marriage, with our children and in our ministry, with amazing results. The basic premise is that we all have core fears, that when triggered, cause us to react in certain ways. Smalley explains:

Without identifying your own core fear and understanding how you act when your fear button gets pushed, your relationships will suffer, every time.

In *Healing Of a Wounded Idealist* we noted that, "of all the things that wound an idealist, nothing is as wounding as relational conflict and disconnect." For this reason, we believe that it is essential for idealists to equip themselves with tools to help them in their relationships.

We approached the Smalley Institute for permission to share

---

[40] Smalley, Gary. The DNA of Relationships. (2007) Tyndale House Publishers,Inc. Used with permission. All rights reserved.

the test with you, and we are very grateful to them for allowing us to do so. Take a few minutes and test yourself.

Core Fears Test

Step One: Identify the Conflict
Take your time as this is key to the test being effective.
- Identify a recent conflict, argument, or negative situation with your spouse, friend, child, neighbour, co-worker, etc., something that really upset you. Think about how you were feeling and how you wished the person would not say or do the things that upset you.

N.B. DON'T CONTINUE WITH THE TEST UNTIL YOU HAVE IDENTIFIED A CONFLICT OR SITUATION. THE REST OF THE TEST IS BASED ON THIS.

Step Two: Identify your Feelings
- How did this conflict or situation make you feel? Mark all that apply but star the most important feelings:

___unsure ___uncomfortable ___frightened
___apathetic ___confused ___anxious
___puzzled ___worried ___horrified
___upset ___disgusted ___disturbed
___sullen ___resentful ___furious
___sad ___bitter ___shamed ___embarrassed
___hurt ___fed up
___disappointed ___frustrated
___wearied ___miserable
___torn up ___guilty ___other

Step Three: Identify Your Fear

- How did this conflict make you feel about yourself? Mark all that apply, but star the TWO most important feelings.

___**rejected** The other person doesn't want me or need me. I am not necessary in this relationship; I feel unwanted.

___**abandoned** The other person will ultimately leave me; I will be left alone to care for myself, the other person won't be committed to me for life.

___**disconnected** We will become emotionally detached or separated; I feel cut off from the other person.

___**like a failure** I am not successful at being a husband/wife, friend, parent, coworker; I will not perform correctly; I will not live up to expectations, I am not good enough.

___**helpless** I cannot do anything to change the other person or my situation; I do not possess the power, resources, capacity, or ability to get what I want; I will feel controlled by the other person.

___**defective** Something is wrong with me; I'm the problem.

___**inadequate** I am not capable; I am incompetent.

___**inferior** Everyone else is better than I am; I am less valuable or important than others.

___**invalidated** Who I am, what I think, what I do, or how I feel is not valued.

___**unloved** The other person doesn't care about me; my relationship lacks warm attachment, admiration, enthusiasm, or devotion.

___**cheated** The other person will take advantage of me or will withhold something I need; I won't get what I want.

___**worthless** I am useless; I have no value to the other person.

___**unaccepted** I am never able to meet the other person's expectations; I am not good enough.

___**unfairly judged** The other person forms faulty or negative opinions about me; I am always being evaluated; the other person does not approve of me.

___**humiliated** The relationship is extremely destructive to my self-respect or dignity.

___**ignored** The other person will not pay attention to me; I feel neglected.

___**insignificant** I am irrelevant in the relationship; the other person does not see me as an important part of our relationship.

Step Four: Identify Your Reactions

- What do you do when you feel (__insert the most important feeling from question number 3)?
- How do you react when you feel that way? Identify your common verbal or physical reactions to deal with that feeling. Check all that apply, but star the TWO most important reactions.

___**withdrawal** you avoid others or alienate yourself without resolution; you sulk or use the silent treatment.

___**escalation** emotions spiral out of control; you argue, raise your voice, fly into a rage.

___**try harder** you try to do more to earn others' love and care.

___**negative beliefs** you believe the other person is far worse than is really the case; you see the other person in a negative light or attribute negative motives to him or her.

___**blaming** you place responsibility on others, not accepting fault; you're convinced the problem is the other person's fault.

___**exaggeration** you make overstatements or enlarge your words beyond bound or the truth.

___**denial** you refuse to admit the truth or reality.

___**invalidation** you devalue the other person; you do not appreciate what he or she feels or thinks or does.

___**defensiveness** instead of listening, you defend yourself by providing an explanation.

___**clinginess** you develop a strong emotional attachment or dependence on the other person.

___**passive-aggressive** you display negative emotions, resentment, and aggression in passive ways, such as procrastination and stubbornness.

___**care-taking** you become responsible for the other person by giving physical or emotional care and support to the point you are doing everything for the other person, who does nothing to care for himself or herself.

___**acting out** you engage in negative behaviors, such as drug or alcohol abuse, extramarital affairs, excessive shopping or spending or overeating.

___**fix-it mode** you focus almost exclusively on what is needed to solve the problem.

___**complaining** you express unhappiness or make accusations, you criticize, create a list of the other person's faults

___**aggression or abuse** you become verbally or physically aggressive, possibly abusive.

___**manipulation** you control the other person for your own advantage, you try to get him or her to do what you want.

___**catastrophize** you use dramatic exaggerated expressions to depict that the relationship is in danger or that it has failed.

___**numbing out** you become devoid of emotions or you have no regard for others' needs or troubles.

___**humor** you use humor as a way of not dealing with the issue at hand.

___**sarcasm** you use negative humor, hurtful words, belittling comments, cutting remarks or demeaning statements.

___**minimization** you assert that the other person is overreacting to an issue; you intentionally underestimate, downplay, or soft-pedal the issue.

___**rationalization** you attempt to make your actions seem reasonable; you try to attribute your behavior to credible motives; you try to provide believable but untrue reasons for your conduct.

___**indifference** you are cold and show no concern.

___**abdication** you give away responsibilities, give up.

___**self-abandonment** you run yourself down; you neglect yourself.

5. Look at the items you starred in response to question three. List the two main feelings.
These are your core fears.

Core fear 1_____

Core fear 2_____

6. Look at the items you starred in response to question four. List your two main reactions.
These are indicators that your core fears have been triggered.

Reaction 1_____

Reaction 2_____

(Figuring out *where* your core fears come from would be another worthwhile exercise in self-awareness, but it is not necessary for the benefits of the test.)

Your core fears may be obvious or a surprise to you. It

certainly helps to recognise how you react when they are triggered. In relationships, Dr. Smalley calls it *The Fear Dance.*

The Fear Dance

Let's say we have a couple, John and Jane.
- John's core fear is rejection and his reaction is to blame.
- Jane's core fear is to be unfairly judged and her reaction is to withdraw.

One day John spontaneously suggests that they go out for dinner and a movie. Jane had already planned to visit a friend in hospital and feels that she cannot cancel. John feels rejected and starts blaming Jane for the lack of closeness in their marriage. This triggers Jane's core fear and she grows quiet. John senses her withdrawal which further triggers his rejection, and expresses his frustration at Jane's inability to express how she feels. This further triggers Jane's fear of being unfairly judged and she withdraws even more. And so it goes, on and on. Before they know it, they go to bed distant and frustrated with each other, wondering what just happened!

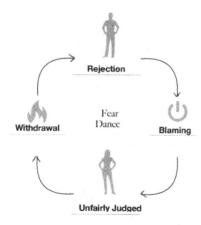

Scenarios like this can play out at work, school, home, with friends and even strangers, without us being aware of why we are being triggered. Becoming self-aware is vital.
But knowing is only half the battle. The key is being able to do something about it.

Take Two

> If we take our newly enlightened couple, the scenario could play out like this. John comes home with his dinner suggestion. Jane knowing that John's core fear is rejection, expresses her excitement at the idea and asks for a rain check till the next day. So far so good, but let's say that John is triggered anyway and starts blaming Jane. He notices that she begins withdrawing. He stops his rant and asks if she feels unfairly judged, which she acknowledges. In a moment of self-awareness, he realises that her postponement made him feel rejected. He says, "Sorry honey, I think I felt rejected by the fact that you wouldn't change your plans." He is able to own his response and feelings, and in turn, she is able to assure him of her love and acceptance.

It sounds simple, and really, it can be. When our son was in primary school, he had a problem with his Math teacher, and his grades started dropping. He had always been a straight A student, so naturally we were concerned. Using the interaction with his teacher as the "conflict situation," we did the core fears test with him. We quickly realised that his core fears were invalidation and being unfairly judged, and his reactions were to abdicate or give up and become indifferent. Irene went in to see the teacher to understand what was going on. The teacher was very strict and had been giving the class detention for talking during lessons. Our son had spoken to the teacher, explaining that he had not been talking. She had told him that it was not her problem, and that everyone would be punished. This went on for a term. When Irene explained that our son was feeling invalidated, the teacher agreed that it would be fair to punish only the students who were talking in class, and let the rest go. Within a few weeks our sons grades were back up, and he hasn't looked back since!

By consistently identifying when our core fears are triggered, we will start to recognise the real issues that are bothering us, instead of allowing ourselves to do and say things we will regret later.

Taking it a Step Further

As Christians, we benchmark our lives to Jesus. He is our model on how to face fear and react. The scriptures reveal that Jesus faced every one of the core fears described above.

Rejected

He was despised and rejected by mankind, a man of suffering, and familiar with pain. Like one from whom people hide their faces he was despised, and we held him in low esteem.[41]

---

[41] Isaiah 53:3

Abandoned

About three in the afternoon Jesus cried out in a loud voice, "Eli, Eli, lema sabachthani?" (which means "My God, my God, why have you forsaken me?" Matthew 27:46

Disconnected

My God, my God, why have you forsaken me? Why are you so far from saving me, so far from my cries of anguish? Psalm 22:1

Inadequate/ defective/ perceived failure

But I am a worm and not a man, scorned by everyone, despised by the people. All who see me mock me; they hurl insults, shaking their heads. "He trusts in the Lord," they say, "let the Lord rescue him. Let him deliver him, since he delights in him." Psalm 22:6

Helpless/unloved/worthless

You know how I am scorned, disgraced and shamed; all my enemies are before you. Scorn has broken my heart and has left me helpless; I looked for sympathy, but there was none, for comforters, but I found none. They put gall in my food and gave me vinegar for my thirst. Psalm 69:19

Inferior/Invalidated/humiliated

Then the governor's soldiers took Jesus into the Praetorium and gathered the whole company of soldiers around him. They stripped him and put a scarlet robe on him, and then twisted together a crown of thorns and set it on his head. They put a staff in his right hand. Then they knelt in front of him and mocked him. "Hail, king of the Jews!" they said. They spat on him, and took the staff and struck him on the head again and again. Matthew 27:27-30

Cheated

He was oppressed and treated harshly, yet he never said a word. He was led like a lamb to the slaughter. And as a sheep is silent before the shearers, he did not open his mouth. Unjustly condemned, he was led away. No one cared that he died without descendants, that his life was cut short in midstream. But he was struck down for the rebellion of my people. But he was buried like a criminal. Isaiah 53:7-9 (NLT)

Unaccepted
Jesus left there and went to his hometown, ...he began to teach in the synagogue, and many who heard him were amazed. "Where did this man get these things?" they asked. "What's this wisdom that has been given him? What are these remarkable miracles he is performing? Isn't this the carpenter? Isn't this Mary's son ...." And they took offense at him. Jesus said to them, "A prophet is not without honor except in his own town, among his relatives and in his own home." Mark 6:1-4

Unfairly Judged
Many of them said, "He is demon-possessed and raving mad. Why listen to him?" John 10:20

Ignored
These people honor me with their lips, but their hearts are far from me. Matthew 15:8
Insignificance
"If the world hates you, keep in mind that it hated me first." John 15:18

Jesus faced it all and understands and empathises with us. He knows the pain of rejection and the difficulty of suffering. He not only sees our hurt, he has *felt* our hurt.

If anyone on earth had a reason to lash out or become cynical, it was Jesus. Talk about being misunderstood, abused, slandered, hated, betrayed. But here's the amazing thing, he never:

47

- Withdrew, yelled, had a fit of rage or tried harder to earn people's acceptance.
- He never started thinking negatively about people or about God.
- He never blamed, exaggerated, threw tantrums, denied what was happening or made others feel invalidated.
- He didn't become defensive or clingy.
- He didn't try to do everything for everybody or try to fix everyone.
- He didn't act out sexually or with drugs, food, alcohol or money.
- He never complained or was manipulative.
- He didn't become numb to those around him or laugh it off.
- He wasn't sarcastic or indifferent. He didn't neglect himself or take revenge.
- He never gave up hope or stopped loving us.

In fact, the crucifixion was the culmination of every core fear that we could ever face in one terrible event. And even then, he forgave and entrusted himself to him who judges justly.[42]
We have a lot to learn from Jesus!

We hope that this exercise has been beneficial to you and that your confidence and respect in our Lord has grown. May we be able to echo King David when he said:

> I sought the Lord, and he answered me; *he delivered me from all my fears.* Those who look to him are radiant; their faces are never covered with shame. Psalm 34:4

---

[42] 1 Peter 2:23

The Disillusioned Idealist

> A dream delayed,
> is not a dream denied.
> R. L White

For a wounded idealist, unresolved disillusionment is the next step towards persistent anger.

disillusionment
dɪsɪˈluːʒ(ə)nm(ə)nt/

a feeling of disappointment resulting from the discovery that something is not as good as one believed it to be.

Disclaimer

This was a difficult chapter for us to write. From the feedback we received, the majority of people who found *Healing of a Wounded Idealist* helpful, fall into this category. The book seemed to help them to put into words what they felt in their hearts, and to recognise the future trajectory of where those feelings were leading them. The reason this chapter was hard to write, was that we really want it to be helpful, and not another source of disillusionment. *The discovery that something is not as good as one believed it to be* certainly applies here! Hopefully, what we share will help.

Disillusionment was something many Biblical heroes experienced, and Moses was no different.

49

Moses asked the Lord, "Why have you brought this trouble on your servant? What have I done to displease you that you put the burden of all these people on me? Did I conceive all these people? Did I give them birth? … I cannot carry all these people by myself; the burden is too heavy for me. If this is how you are going to treat me, please go ahead and kill me."[43]

When the Dream Becomes a Nightmare

Moses was tired. He felt burdened by the responsibility and reality of leading the Israelites. Maybe he had dreamt about what it would be like to bring the Israelites out of Egypt and form them into a nation, with a divine set of laws to govern them. Perhaps he had imagined their gratitude and awe at being God's chosen people; but human nature being what it is, and people being who they are, the dream quickly became more of a nightmare. What he came to realise was that it had been easier to get the Israelites out of Egypt, than to get Egypt out of the Israelites.[44]

In *Healing of a Wounded Idealist*, we looked at the state of the world and the age-old question of suffering. We considered the disillusioning nature of mankind's journey on earth and proposed some purpose to all the craziness. We will not repeat the discussion here. What we do want to address, is the disillusionment idealists can feel with the church and Christian relationships. The let-down, hurt and disappointment we can feel with leaders and members alike.

---

[43] Numbers11:11-15

[44] www.unfathomablegrace.com/2014/02/28/it-is-easier-to-get-israel-out-of-egypt-than-egypt-out-of-israel/

To get us started, we want to offer a *different* definition of disillusionment:

disillusionment
dɪsɪˈluːʒ(ə)nm(ə)nt/

the state of being free of illusions, of false impressions, or of misconceptions.

Dis-illusionment, the state of living without illusions. The ability to see and perceive things clearly without obstruction; to be able to think with clarity.

What an outstanding notion!

The early twentieth-century preacher Oswald Chambers described this kind of disillusionment as coming from God.

The disillusionment that comes from God brings us to the point where we see people as they really are, yet without any cynicism or any stinging and bitter criticism.
Refusing to be disillusioned is the cause of much of the suffering of human life.[45]

When we consider this definition, then perhaps disillusionment is not a step away from faith after all!
Could it be that a disillusionment from God is just what we need to deepen our faith?
What if God is trying to remove spiritual cataracts from our eyes; attempting to take away the misguided illusions that blur our spiritual vision? Perhaps in order to see him more clearly, we need to see life as it is, and people as they are.

---

[45] www.utmost.org/the-teaching-of-disillusionment/

To understand this better, we will need to answer three questions.

- Why illusions?
- What illusions does God want to take away?
- How do we go forward in faith?

1. Why Illusions?

An illusion refers to either something *that is not as it appears or a misperception*. It is different from a lie, in as much as a magician's illusion is different to falsifying information on a tax return. If the opposite of a lie is truth, the opposite of an illusion would be reality.

The Bible clearly says that all lies come from Satan. He is the father of lies, and his aim is to deceive us and keep us from the truth.[46] Conversely, it is impossible for God to lie.[47] In him, there is no darkness at all. But there are times, when God will allow us to live under an illusion because it serves his purpose. For example, when Moses set out to rescue the Israelites, he was under the illusion that it would be relatively easy. With Aaron as his spokesman, the ability to turn water into blood, a staff that changed into a snake, and God on his side, how difficult would it really be? And God allowed him to live under this illusion. Before Moses left on his mission, God did not go into graphic detail about every obstacle Moses would face over the next 40 years. If he had, we don't think Moses would have gone anywhere near Egypt!

---

[46] John 8:44

[47] Hebrews 6: 18

It can be the same for the idealist and the church.

> For instance, when an idealist is brand new in the faith,
> everything seems so perfect. The leaders seem to have
> all the answers and to be living perfect lives. People
> who are older in the faith, appear to be Bible scholars.
> The worship is magical and the sermons are life-
> changing. For the young Christian idealist in pursuit of
> the ideal, the church, *at first glance*, fits the bill.
> Now, we think that we can all agree that this
> experience of perfection, is an illusion. But, this
> illusion, *at least for idealists*, may well be a necessary
> part of finding their feet in the faith.
> Imagine if the first time you walked into church, you
> were able to see every mistake or fault there was to be
> seen. While a realist may be able to handle it, a young
> idealists' faith may not survive the onslaught of reality.
> So God, in his mercy and wisdom, slowly exposes
> things, as we mature, and only as much as our faith can
> handle.

In this sense, getting to a point of spiritual maturity where God
feels you are ready to be disillusioned is actually a spiritual pat
on the back. A "well done," if you may. "You are mature
enough to know the truth." It's like when a child has matured
enough to realise that the tooth fairy doesn't exist. The illusion
may have suited the child for a time, but now it's time to move
on to maturity. In a similar way, a disillusionment from God is
a call to mature, to grow and to see things more clearly.

(But we can be sure of this, events that tear away illusions are painful.[48] Some have experienced the pain of this disillusionment, and have become stuck in it for months, even years. This is not what God intended. It is time to move on to deeper faith.)

If we want to have a clear spiritual vision, we need to allow a disillusionment from God.

2. What illusions does God want to take away?

Let's start with an obvious one, and go from there.

> The Bible calls us to respect and hold in the highest regard those who are over us in the Lord.[49] And this is good and right. But it is an illusion to think that leaders are faultless or do not make mistakes. (They are saved sinners, just like the rest of us.) While this illusion may be helpful for a time, if we don't grow from under it, we run the risk of going beyond respecting leaders, to idolising them, and making them into spiritual celebrities. We may end up setting our hope on them, rather than on God. This will prove to be *very* disappointing! We must allow God to remove this illusion from our spiritual eyes. (The trick from there, is to find the grace to see our leaders clearly, warts and all, and yet in mercy and humility, afford them the

---

[48] Especially at the hand of other Christians. We encourage you to read the book, *Crucified by Christians,* by Gene Edwards. Seedsowers Publishers

[49] 1 Thessalonians 5:12-13 We ask you, brothers, to respect those who labor among you and are over you in the Lord and admonish you. Hold them in the highest regard in love because of their work

respect God calls us to have. This same mutual acceptance applies to all spiritual relationships.)

Idealists enjoy illusions. It helps them create an alternative reality to the harsh world they see around them. But spiritually, there is a danger in choosing an illusion over reality.
Below is a list of ten things idealists can have a misperception about. We'll call it a reality checklist.

Illusion	Reality
God's mission always feels fulfilling	Exodus 5: 22-23, Psalm 43, Jeremiah 8:4-6, Ezekiel 3:14-15
My identity is tied up with my economic status, race, education, and gender	Galatians 3:26-28, 1 John 3:1 Colossians 3:1-3 Philippians 3: 3-8,
I am in control of my life	Proverbs19:21, Proverbs16:9, James 4:13-14, Job 34:14-15
I am meant to "save" the world. God and others expect this of me.	2 Corinthians 4:5, 2 Timothy 2:15-19. Not even the saviour had a saviour complex, John 6:60-67
If God is pleased with me, then he won't let me suffer	Matthew 3:17-4:1, Job 23:10, 1 Peter 4:12-16
The church is there to meet all my needs	Philippians 2:3-4, Ephesians 4:16, 1 Corinthians 12:12-16
Godly people should not struggle with depression	Psalm 42:11, Job 3:11 Jeremiah 20:14-18, Psalm 34:18
I can learn to obey without suffering or discomfort	Hebrews 5:8, Hebrews 12:4-11, Deuteronomy 8:2-5

Illusion	Reality
If I pray in faith, then I will get whatever I ask for.	1 John 5:14, James 4:3 James 4:13-16
I shouldn't be hurt or let down by people in the church	Ephesians 4:2-3 Colossians 3:12-13
God can only be glorified when I am strong	2 Corinthians 12:8-10 1 Corinthians 2:3-5

We encourage you to take the time to study out these scriptures, and to make up your own list.

Once we recognise the illusions we are living under, we can then move forward in faith. And again, we turn to Moses to show us a path ahead.

3. Moving Forward in Faith

The book of Deuteronomy records Moses' final instructions to the Israelites before they crossed the Jordan River into the Promised Land. After 40 years of wandering in the wilderness, the next generation of Israel was finally old enough to enter Canaan. The adult Israelites who would enter Canaan were not the same ones that had left Egypt. God had loved, led, provided for and guided the former generation but they had refused to submit to him. Psalm 78 documents the wilderness ordeal, summing it up like this:

>...they did not believe in God
>or trust in his deliverance. Psalm 78:22

Moses knew that this new generation had much to learn going forward, but he also wanted them to have the right perspective of the things they had already been through. (It's easy to endure difficult times without asking what lesson God might be trying to teach you. What we have realised after 30 years, when God wants to teach you something, no matter how many times you try to avoid it, the lesson will be repeated until you learn what you need to. Best to learn quickly!)

The Israelites needed to remember the lessons they had learnt, but Moses also wanted to spare them from the potential disillusionment they were sure to experience as they entered the promised land.

> Think for a moment what must have been going through their minds as they stood at the edge of a new dawn. This was a people who had been in captivity for 400 years and within a generation, they had been set free, and promised their own land, flocks, fields and herds. Everything they could have ever wanted or dreamed about.

But there is an illusion to having it all. Moses had once had it all when he lived as a prince of Egypt. Over time he had learned that God was the one behind all his royal opportunities, and all for a God-ordained purpose, and not self-gratification. Moses wanted these Israelites to realise that it was an illusion to think that they would be the ones creating their own success in this new land. God had brought them this far, and God would be the one to help them succeed; and all for his divine purpose.

When you have eaten and are satisfied, praise the Lord your God for the good land *he has given you*. Be careful that you do not forget the Lord your God, failing to observe his commands, his laws and his decrees that I am giving you this day. Otherwise, when you eat and are satisfied, when you build fine houses and settle down, and when your herds and flocks grow large and your silver and gold increase and all you have is multiplied, then your heart will become proud and you will forget the Lord your God, *who brought you* out of Egypt, out of the land of slavery. *He led you* through the vast and dreadful wilderness, that thirsty and waterless land, with its venomous snakes and scorpions. *He brought you* water out of hard rock. *He gave you* manna to eat in the wilderness, to humble and test you so that in the end it might go well with you. You may say to yourself, "My power and the strength of my hands have produced this wealth for me." But remember the Lord your God, for *it is he who gives you the ability* to produce wealth, and **so confirms his covenant**, which he swore to your ancestors. Deuteronomy 8:10-18

Without the Israelites coming out from under the illusion that they would be the ones to create their own success, the next step would be pride and forgetting God.

When God attempts to take away our illusions, we have a choice to make. Every choice we make will come with its own next steps and consequences. There are always next steps when we refuse a disillusionment from God, and it can be the same with idealists and illusions about the church, marriage, parenting, relationships, money, etc.

The following chart is one example of what it may look like:

Illusion 1: The church is a perfect place.

Disillusioning Event - Let down by people in the church.

CHOICE

Embrace the reality.
Next Steps: 2 Peter 1: 3-9

Deepen your faith and trust in God. Stand in awe that God uses weak people, (including yourself) to do his will on earth. Express your concerns constructively. Roll up your sleeves, help out. Use your talents to build up the church. Live a life of repentance.

Rather than be disillusioned and recognise the call to maturity, you choose an: **Alternative reality.**
Illusion 2: I am a good person. My heart and thoughts are right before God, even if others aren't.
Next Step: Either become a victim of circumstance, or the defender of the "weak," protecting others from being hurt by the church.

Disillusioning Event - Your sin is exposed and you realise that you are a sinner with issues you need to deal with in your own heart and life.

CHOICE

Embrace the reality.
Next Steps:
Deepen your faith and trust in God. Stand in awe that God uses weak people, (including yourself) to do his will on earth. Express your concerns constructively. Roll up your sleeves, help out. Use your talents to build up the church. Live a life of repentance.

Illusion 3: Being a Christian is too hard and the expectations of the church are too unrealistic.
Next Step
- Find alternatives fixes. Eg Change leadership roles, house churches, etc
- Create groups to vent frustrations and criticism.
- Focus on own culture above Christian culture.
- Change your doctrine to suit your lifestyle.

Disillusioning Event - others aren't as excited or convinced about the "obvious fixes". You don't feel heard or understood.

CHOICE

Embrace the reality.
Next Steps:
Deepen your faith and trust in God. Stand in awe that God uses weak people, (including yourself) to do his will on earth. Express your concerns constructively. Roll up your sleeves, help out. Use your talents to build up the church. Live a life of repentance.

Illusion 4: We are all spiritual beings and God is not limited to one place. We commune with God through nature and spirit and a church community is not necessary.
Next Step:
- Leave the church or start a new group.
- Let go of sound doctrine
- Judge/speak negatively of those who stay.

Without allowing God to remove the obstructions from our eyes, to see *ourselves* and others more clearly, the final step will end in spiritual blindness! And the irony of spiritual blindness, is that those living in it, insist that they have been enlightened. The illusion has become a lie.

Peter put it like this:

Make every effort to add to your faith goodness; and to goodness, knowledge; and to knowledge, self-control; and to self-control, perseverance; and to perseverance, godliness; and to godliness, mutual affection; and to mutual affection, love. For if you possess these qualities in increasing measure, they will keep you from being ineffective and unproductive in your knowledge of our Lord Jesus Christ. ***But whoever does not have them is nearsighted and blind, forgetting that they have been cleansed from their past sins.*** 2 Peter 1:5-9

THE BRIDGE OF HUMILITY

In light of what we have just studied, we ask you to consider a few things :

1. Choose to submit to God and not resist what he is trying to teach you. Ask yourself: what do I need to learn from this?
2. Trust that Jesus *is* the head of the church[50] — and that he knowingly uses flawed people to lead other flawed people. He knows that it's not perfect.
   - He sees and knows everything; including the thoughts in your heart.
   - He raises people up, and can just as easily remove

---

50 Colossians 1:18

them. Remember, Judas had the perfect leader, adviser, and counsellor, and yet did terribly spiritually. Samuel had a horrible spiritual upbringing in Eli's house, yet became a mighty man of God.

- Choose to use your gifts and talents to build up the church. Speak up and use your voice to help the church and not to break it down.

3. Write up your own Disillusionment Chart, based on disillusionment(s) with your: marriage, having/raising children, finding the perfect spouse, career, etc., and the choices you have made.

A disillusionment from God should lead us to greater faith than we have ever known, as we recognise that *with God*:

> Things can be perfect,
> even when they are not.[51]

---

[51] Unknown source

Biblical Promises
for the humble

The Lord **saves** the humble - Psalm 18:27

The Lord **guides** the humble in what is right - Psalm 25:9

The Lord **teaches** the humble his way - Psalm 25:9

The Lord **sustains** the humble - Psalm 147:6

The Lord **crowns** the humble **with victory** - Psalm 149:4

The Lord **hears** the humble - Daniel 10:12

The Lord **is mindful of** the humble - Luke 1:48

The Lord **exalts** the humble - Luke 14:11

The Lord **lifts up** the humble - James 4:10

The Lord **shows favour to** the humble - 1 Peter 5:5

The Discouraged Idealist

*Sometimes courage is the quiet
voice at the end of the day saying,
"I will try again tomorrow."*
MJ Radmacher

As we continue back through the steps of wounding, we reach discouragement. For an idealist, persistent discouragement is the step before becoming disillusioned.

discouragement
/dɪsˈkʌrɪdʒm(ə)nt/

a loss of confidence or enthusiasm.

Common Causes

Fatigue : When you're physically or emotionally exhausted, you're a prime candidate for discouragement. Your defences are lowered and things can seem bleaker than they really are.

Frustration: When unfinished tasks pile up, it's natural to feel overwhelmed. And when trivial matters interrupt and prevent you from accomplishing what you really need to do, your frustration can easily produce discouragement.

Failure: Sometimes, your best-laid plans fall apart, the

project collapses, the deal falls through or no one shows up to an event. Struggling in relationships, finances, or with illness can cause discouragement. Seeing others suffer can be equally distressing for an idealist.[52]

Spiritual Cause For Discouragement

Moses returned to the Lord and said, "Why, Lord, why have you brought trouble on this people? Is this why you sent me? Ever since I went to Pharaoh to speak in your name, he has brought trouble on this people, and you have not rescued your people at all." Exodus 5:22-23

Moses was discouraged. He had met God in the Midian Desert and been given a plan to get the Israelites out of Egypt, a staff that transformed into a snake, the ability to turn his hand leprous, and a spokesman in his older brother, Aaron. All this so that the Israelites would believe that God had sent him.

It had taken a while for God to convince Moses of the mission, and as he strode towards Egypt, Moses knew that the Israelites would take some persuading too. What he hadn't anticipated, was that Pharaoh would pose such a problem! Far from being rescued, his request to Pharaoh to allow the Israelites to worship in the desert for three days, had resulted in them having to make bricks with less straw!

Moses was losing confidence in himself, the plan and in God. It was still early on in his mission, but it discouraged him deeply.

---

[52]www.pastors.com/4-causes-of-discouragement-and-4-cures/

Do Not Be Discouraged

Although Moses had been extremely discouraged, over time, he figured out its source. As he passed the mantle on to Joshua, he charged him with these words:

The Lord himself goes before you and will be with you; he will never leave you nor forsake you. **Do not be afraid; do not be discouraged**. Deuteronomy 31:8

God repeated the words to Joshua after Moses' death:

Have I not commanded you? Be strong and courageous. **Do not be afraid; do not be discouraged**, for the Lord your God will be with you wherever you go. Joshua 1:9

Over and over again, when the Bible gives the charge to not be discouraged, there is always another statement attached;
"Do not be afraid."
(See: Joshua 8:1, Joshua 10:25, 1 Chronicles 28:20,
2 Chronicles 20:15-17, 2 Chronicles 32:7.)

The Bible teaches that discouragement and fear go hand in hand. When we are afraid, we can easily become discouraged. In a way, it makes sense, since the root word of discouragement is to have, "no more courage."

No More Courage

We all know what it feels like to lose courage. Where the confidence you felt about the choices you were making, and the way in which you were building your life, relationships and future, falters, leaving you unsure.

If we apply what we have just learned about the spiritual source of discouragement, we will hopefully find a way through it. Let's start by saying: Don't make big decisions on bad days. Instead, ask yourself: What has caused me to *lose my courage*?

Maybe it is:
- Loneliness? Maybe you fear never finding "the one," or if you are in a relationship or marriage, you fear that you will be rejected.
- Failure? Maybe it's something you failed at recently? A relationship that didn't work out, or a job you didn't get or were let go from?
- Disappointment with someone? Has someone you love lost their faith or have friends you respected and admired been unfaithful to one another? Has a leader not been what you expected?
- Fear of not being good enough or of not being capable? Do you fear that you don't have impact, or are ineffective?
- Death or illness? Are you or someone you love, ill? Are you afraid of what the future holds in regard to your health or your loved one's health?
- Financial stress? Have you lost courage and hope when it comes to your finances and financial future? Are you in a lot of debt?
- Fear that what you are working towards will come to nothing? That the hours of effort, time and energy you invest in relationships, ministry and career will be futile.
- Fear of hoping? That though dreams can come true, you have experienced that they can just as easily become nightmares.

- Fear of aging? Maybe you fear that you will live till old age and become "decrepit" and a burden on your family, or that you will be alone and unwanted.
- Fear for your children? Their salvation, health and future.

Fear can literally suck the courage out of us. Take a moment to recognise (and write down) what you have lost courage about.

I Am With You

Now that we know what causes discouragement, we need to know what we can do about it? How do you regain courage? What can make us brave again?

To find the answer, we must go back to the very same Scriptures[53] we have just read.

> **The Lord** himself goes before you and **will be with you**; he will never leave you nor forsake you. Do not be afraid; do not be discouraged. Deuteronomy 31:8

> Have I not commanded you? Be strong and courageous. Do not be afraid; do not be discouraged, for **the Lord your God will be with you** wherever you go. Joshua 1:9

No matter what you are going through right now, God is saying, "I am with you!"

- You can be strong and courageous.
- God is saying, "I am with you, so you can face the future with courage." You can trust the Scripture when it says your

---

[53] Joshua 8:1, Joshua 10:25, 1 Chronicles 28:20, 2 Chronicles 20:15-17, 2 Chronicles 32:7

labour in the Lord is not in vain[54] and that God will not forget your work and the love you have shown him as you have helped his people.[55]

- The creator of the universe has got your back.
- Your heavenly Father is on your side. God doesn't have grandchildren or nieces and nephews, he only has children and you are one of them. He is always there, by your side.
- You are not alone.
- You don't have to fight the battles of life on your own.
- You don't have to struggle by yourself.

Sometimes we act as if we are alone, that we leave God when we finish praying in the morning. But he is with you in the car, in the traffic, at home, at work, at school, in the shops… wherever you are, he is there. He is always with you.

Before we think that this promise only applies to Old Testament times, let us remember Jesus' words as he left earth:

> Then Jesus came to them and said, "All authority in heaven and on earth has been given to me. Therefore go and make disciples of all nations, baptising them in the name of the Father and of the Son and of the Holy Spirit, and teaching them to obey everything I have commanded you. And surely I am with you always, to the very end of the age."
> Matthew 28:18-20

Jesus tells us that he will be with us always. Day after day after day, right up to the end of the age. God is with us, Jesus is with us, let us get our eyes off of what makes us afraid and trust God

---

[54] 1 Corinthians 15:58

[55] Hebrews 6:10

with our futures and our families, our hopes and dreams. Let us rather get busy fulfilling the great commission that he has called each of us to.

THE BRIDGE OF HUMILITY

- Take some time to figure out what has taken away your courage. Try and pinpoint when you started feeling discouraged.
- Get some encouragement. The book of Hebrews tells us to:

  Encourage one another daily, as long as it is called Today, so that none of you may be hardened by sin's deceitful.[56]

- We need daily encouragement in our lives. In the busyness of life, it is easy to become independent and self-reliant. But God has designed us to need each other, to live in community and to receive and give encouragement. Life is tough, we cannot do this alone. Call a friend.
- Finally, remember that you are not alone. God is with you. He wants to encourage you.

  You, Lord, hear the desire of the afflicted;
  you encourage them, and you listen to their cry.
  Psalm 10:17

Take courage Idealist, it's going to be ok.

---

[56] Hebrews 3:12-13

Patience

My problem is this; I am in
a hurry, and God is not.
P. Brooks

patience
/ˈpeɪʃ(ə)ns/

*the capacity to accept or tolerate delay, problems,
or suffering without becoming annoyed or anxious.*

Waiting patiently for an idealist, is hard. Really, really hard!
When an idealist imagines something he or she believes needs
to done or said, it becomes a matter of urgency. And being
prudent (to act or show care and thought for the future), is not
one of an idealist's greatest strengths!

As a young man in Egypt, Moses had watched his people be
mistreated. He had seen the beatings and the cruelty of the
slave drivers. Maybe he prayed that God would show him what
to do, but God had remained silent. Day after day, the anger
and frustration at the injustice, and of not being able to do
anything, grew, until one day he had had enough of waiting.

One day, after Moses had grown up, he went out to where his
own people were and watched them at their hard labor. He
saw an Egyptian beating a Hebrew, one of his own people.
Looking this way and that and seeing no one, he killed the
Egyptian and hid him in the sand. Exodus 2:11-12

Moses may have reasoned that God was waiting for him to do

something, so checking to make sure that no one was looking, he killed an Egyptian taskmaster and buried the evidence. It seemed like a good idea at the time, but his rashness cost him dearly.

Why aren't you doing anything, God?

Moses' problem was that he made the mistake of believing that God wasn't going to act, and so he needed to. An idealist's impatience can cause him or her to do the same. When an idealist believes that God isn't seeing a problem or listening to their requests, they can end up taking matters into their own hands.

Problem	Rash decision	Consequence	Regret
I don't like my job. I need a new one now.	I am going to quit, even though I don't have another job lined up.	It's harder than I imagined to find a new one.	I wish I had my old job, I can't pay my rent.
I need a car now	Purchase a new car.	The payments, insurance and upkeep are more than I imagined.	I hate my new car.
I need a boyfriend/ girlfriend now	I will go out and find one, even if we don't share the same Biblical standards.	I need to confess impurity.	This can't be what God has planned for me.

Problem	Rash decision	Consequence	Regret
I want a pet now	Buy a dog that looked so cute on Instagram.	Owning a pet is more work than I realised.	I feel so burdened by the responsibility.
I need to be successful now	Over work and over schedule yourself.	I feel sick and exhausted all the time.	I feel disconnected from God and others.
I need to buy a house or TV, or furniture, clothing, an exotic holiday etc. now	Buys one or more items on credit or uses up savings.	I have used up my savings and credit, and now am in a lot of debt.	The financial stress and pressure I feel are making me sick.
I need...now			

You can fill in your own list.

None of the things above are wrong, but sometimes, out of a sense of desperation, we can end up doing things that make us more miserable than we were, and then do another rash thing to get out of our new situation. And so the cycle repeats itself.

THE BRIDGE OF HUMILITY

Be Still

> Be still, and know that I am God
> Psalm 40:10

Jewish writer, J. Parsons, gives a fresh perspective on this familiar verse:

The command to "be still" comes from the verb *rapha,* which means to be weak, to let go, or to release. It might be better translated as, "cause yourselves to let go" or "let yourselves become weak." But to what end are we to "be still, or let go"? In Hebrew grammar, the emphasis of coordinate imperatives is on the second imperative ("be still!" and **"know!"**).

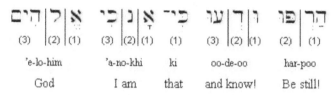

הַרְפּוּ	וּדְעוּ	כִּי־אָנֹכִי	אֱלֹהִים
(2) (1)	(3) (2) (1)	(1) (3) (2) (1)	(3) (2) (1)
har-poo	oo-de-oo	ki ʼa-no-khi	ʼe-lo-him
Be still!	and know!	that I am	God

In other words, we surrender *in order to* know that God is in control. We "let go" *in order* to objectively know the saving power of God in our lives. We give up trusting in ourselves and our own designs in order to experience the glory of God's all-sufficiency.[57]

What an insight! God is not calling us to be still and know/believe/trust that he is God. No, he calls us to be still *so that* he can show us that he is God. Be still in order to know that he is God. He *places the onus on himself* to "prove" that he is God. What he requires of us is to be still!

In the New Testament, Jesus gives us the same encouragement with the assurance that God knows what we need:

So do not worry, saying, 'What shall we eat?' or 'What shall we drink?' or 'What shall we wear?' For the pagans run after all these things, and your heavenly Father knows that you need them. But seek first his kingdom and his righteousness, and all these things will be given to you as well. Therefore do not

---

[57] John J. Parsons.www.hebrew4christians.com/Meditations/Be_Still

worry about tomorrow, for tomorrow will worry about itself. Each day has enough trouble of its own. Mathew 6:31-33

Rather than taking matters into our own hands and meeting our own needs, we need to be still and let God work out the details of our lives.

Trust in God's Timing

From the basic needs of our lives, to important decisions throughout our lives, we need to learn to trust God's timing. Let's look at a couple examples, starting with our man Moses:

Moses answered the people, "Do not be afraid. Stand firm and you will see the deliverance the Lord will bring you today. The Egyptians you see today you will never see again. The Lord will fight for you; you need only to be still." Then the Lord said to Moses, "Why are you crying out to me? Tell the Israelites to move on. Raise your staff and stretch out your hand over the sea to divide the water so that the Israelites can go through the sea on dry ground. Exodus 14:13-16

- Moses had learned the lesson to be still and wait for God. The Israelites were pinned between the Egyptian army and the Red Sea, but rather than be rash, Moses encourages them to be still. Ironically, this time God tells him to move on. It was time to act!
- We can even see the different perspectives about when was the right time to act between Jesus and his brothers:

  Jesus' brothers said to him, "Leave Galilee and go to Judea, so that your disciples there may see the works you do. No one who wants to become a public figure acts in secret. Since you are doing these things, show yourself to the world." For even his own brothers did not believe in him. Therefore Jesus told them, "My time is not yet here; *for you any time will do*.[58]

- Regarding dating and marriage, there is a right time:

    Do not arouse or awaken love until *the time is right*.[59]

- In becoming a person of impact or influence in your sphere of life or work, there is a right time:

    Humble yourselves, therefore, under the mighty hand of God so that *at the proper time* he may exalt you. 1 Peter 5:6

- Even the time for saving our souls was carefully determined by God:

    You see, at *just the right time*, when we were still powerless, Christ died for the ungodly. Romans 5:6

The point is, there is a right time. God's time, and it's perfect. If we will quiet our souls and minds, God will make his timing known. Yes, we need to do our part, but all the while trusting that God will do his part, at the right time. Don't take matters into your own hands.

Everyday Practicals

If you struggle with impatience, we encourage you to pray daily for God to help you to grow in patience. But in the meantime, here are a few practicals to help you in your

---

[58] John 7:3-6

[59] Song of Songs 2:7(NLT)

everyday interactions.

- Train yourself to give **thanks in every circumstance**.[60] Thank God for the delays. Thank him for teaching you to wait and be patient.
- **Expect** things to take longer than you imagined. Plan extra days or hours for getting something done.
- Don't give yourself or others idealistic/unrealistic deadlines.
- When you are stuck in a queue that is taking a long time, rather than getting frustrated, say to yourself, "It is what it is." Take a deep breath. Look around for someone you can encourage or share the gospel with, instead of complaining.
- **Accept** that life is full of difficulties and delays, it's one of the curses from the Garden of Eden.[61]
- Be as patient with others as you would like them to be with you.
- **Be prudent** in your decision making. We regularly remind each other that our "older selves" will thank us for the prudent decisions we are making today.

We need to learn to wait for the Lord.

Wait for the Lord; be strong and take heart
and wait for the Lord. Psalm 27:14

God doesn't need our help but he does want to help us. We must obey his word and wait for him. Idealist, it is better to wait a while and have things fall into place than to rush and have things fall apart.

---

[60] 1 Thessalonians 5:16

[61] Genesis 3:17-18

The Disappointed Idealist

We must accept finite disappointment,
but never lose infinite hope.
Martin Luther King, Jr.

disappointment
/dɪsəˈpɔɪntm(ə)nt/

sadness or displeasure caused by the
non-fulfilment of one's hopes or expectations.

Unfortunately for idealists, disappointment is inevitable. With their idealistic expectations of life, people, and even of God, reality is unavoidably disappointing.

In an attempt to circumvent feeling let down by reality, idealists are in a constant state of striving for their ideal world. Their hearts and minds are restless. They strive for the perfect relationships, boyfriend, girlfriend, spouse, government, society, varsity, career, job, car, house, neighbourhood, personality, character strengths, and church experience. And the striving can feel endless. They go from one thing to another, convinced that if they can just have this ONE thing then life will be right and they will be at peace. But the peace or satisfaction received from getting or achieving something is often short lived and the striving continues. Peace remains just out of reach.

To make matters worse, young idealists can feel entitled to certain things that they feel God, life, the world, their parents or others owe them. They are further disappointed when they don't receive these things or are expected to have to work for them.

A Necessary Apology

Modern society has set these young idealists up for disappointment. In an attempt to be inclusive and make everyone feel special, society has inadvertently coddled these young idealists and tried to shelter them from the harsh realities of life. In Ecclesiastes, Solomon reminds us that:

> The fastest runner doesn't always win the race, and the strongest warrior doesn't always win the battle. The wise sometimes go hungry, and the skilful are not necessarily wealthy. And those who are educated don't always lead successful lives.[62]

Psychologist Wendy Mogel, said it well when she said:

> Our job is to prepare our children for the road, and not the road for our children.[63]

Sadly, all too often, this has not happened. And to the young idealists surprised at how hard life can be, we say sorry! We should have taught you better. We should have let you experience the consequences of your decisions instead of

---

[62] Ecclesiastes 9:11(NLT)

[63] The Blessing of a Skinned Knee: Using Jewish Teachings to Raise Self-Reliant Children. Wendy Mogel. Penguin Books. 2001.

rescuing you. We should have allowed you to learn the benefit of suffering and the principle of reaping and sowing. Our bad! Prayerfully we will all do better going forward. As a way to help, we have included in the appendix, a comprehensive list of everything that God and life owe you. We encourage you to familiarise yourself with it. It will help you to manage your expectations and future disappointment.

THE BRIDGE OF HUMILITY

While disappointment for an idealist is inevitable, we do believe that there are ways for a young idealist to approach life with a more sober outlook and learn to manage disappointment in ways that do not damage faith. In order to do this, he or she must:

- Deal with People Pleasing
- Overcome Insecurity
- Choose Contentment.

1. Approval Addiction

To lessen the sting of disappointment, idealists must deal with their need to please people. Truthfully, it is hard to be really good at something and not feel the need to let the world know about it. But for an idealist, the need for approval is more than just an ego trip; it's an external source of motivation and encouragement. It feels as necessary as food and water. While a realist may recognise that people are fickle and that you cannot make everybody happy, an idealist's mood or day can be seriously influenced by the praise he or she receives or *doesn't receive*. It's almost as if acknowledgement from others validates their actions.

For idealists, if people don't recognise what they have done, or said, or posted, or photographed, or been involved in, then it holds no value. If someone doesn't applaud or give kudos, then it holds no merit. That's why "likes" on Facebook, Instagram, Twitter, etc., hold so much weight. It says, "you're ok, you are accepted, you are approved."

The problem is that these temporary highs don't satisfy but rather increase the need for more and greater acknowledgement. Proverbs 29:25 says that:

> The fear of man will prove to be a snare.

The Message translation puts it like this:

> Fear of human opinion will disable you.

People pleasing is a snare, a trap. It will disable you, limit you and hold you back from the life you desire, and the plans God has for you.

> Am I now trying to win the approval of human beings, or of God? Or am I trying to please people? If I were still trying to please people, I would not be a servant of Christ.
> Galatians 1:10

We cannot serve both God and our desire for people's approval. We will find our Christian walk wrought with anxiety and stress. It's miserable! Being a people pleaser will set you up for so much disappointment, because people are constantly changing. What is cool today is not cool tomorrow. It can be very confusing, but the good news is that there is a different path to take.

Firstly, find your validation in God.

validation
/valɪˈdeɪʃ(ə)n/

*recognition or affirmation that a person or their
feelings or opinions are valid or worthwhile.*

Your value was determined at the cross. Nothing that has happened or will happen in your life will ever change that. It has been determined, signed, sealed and delivered. The God of heaven and earth, of time, space and every other dimension, *thinks that you are worth it.* But you may say, "I don't feel worthy or valuable." Maybe this illustration will be a helpful visual aid:

> Imagine we offered you a $100 bill. Would you want it? Yes? Now imagine we crumpled it up and stood on it. Would you still want it? Yes, why? Because no matter how crumpled or dirty the bill gets, it does not decrease in value. Its value was determined at the time of printing.

Our value was determined at the cross, long before we were born. We don't need to run after validation from people. We have our Father's validation. We have nothing to prove. This is not a competition. Satan is constantly trying to get us to compete with one another or compare ourselves to other people. And comparison can break our spirits because each of us is on our own path. It has been well said:

The comparison trap tricks us into thinking that God's blessings (and validation) are in limited supply, whispering the lie that when someone else wins, you lose.[64]

Rather than feeling threatened by others' success, we should celebrate with them. We are all God's sons and daughters, created by him for his glory.

> Bring my sons from afar and my daughters from the ends of the earth—everyone who is called by my name, **whom I created for my glory**, whom I formed and made.[65]

God wants you, and has a very specific plan and purpose for your life. We are all different. We have been given different talents, gifts, strengths and weaknesses for the path God has chosen for us. Let God be the one to validate you.

Secondly, walk in the light

The second way that we can deal with our people pleasing is by making a deliberate decision to walk in the light. Both Irene and I, made the decision early on in our Christian walks that we would strive to "look our worst before people, so that we could be our best before God."

In James 5:16, the Bible says we are to confess our sins to *each other* and pray for each other. That is humbling, but so beneficial! Not only do others praying for us, but by confessing our sins, we avoid the trap of putting ourselves or others on spiritual pedestals. We recognise that we are all spiritual beggars in desperate need of God's grace. (Also read 1 John 1: 5-10 and Proverbs 28:13.)

---

64 Unknown author

65 Isaiah 43:6-8

2. Overcome Insecurity

Idealists are great dreamers, but can also be given to insecurity. Although they have vision, many times, they lack the confidence to act. This can be a source of disappointment and frustration for an idealist.

Insecurity is tricky. It is defined as, *uncertainty or anxiety about oneself; or as having a lack of confidence.*
Have you ever walked into a room full of strangers who seem to know each other and are not particularly interested in you? Then you know what insecurity feels like. You feel awkward in your own skin; self-conscious, and out of place. You may imagine what people are thinking or saying about you. You long to get out of the situation, or at least find someone you recognise. While a realist might think, "this is to be expected, I am the stranger," and make the best of the situation, for an idealist it can be very disheartening!

So what do you do with insecurity? It's hard to deal with a feeling or give yourself a pep talk. If it grips you to the extreme it can feel like drowning, and can be a big incentive for people to avoid new social situations.

As Christians we deal with things from a spiritual perspective:

Find The Root

So what is the root of insecurity?
- Some say it is pride: having an ego, a reputation to uphold, or wanting people to see you in a certain way.
- Some say it is selfishness: you are focussed on yourself,

on how you are feeling and what you are thinking.
- Some would say it is fear: fear of what people think of you or say about you or that they won't accept or like you.

We agree! The root of insecurity is all of the above.

In some situations it may come from pride and in others it may come from selfishness or fear. So here's where it gets tricky: when you feel insecure, you have to deal with all three roots in order to overcome.

We know that the opposite of pride is humility, the opposite of selfishness is selflessness, and the opposite of fear is courage. So in order to deal with your insecurity you have to be humble, selfless and courageous. Or you could just LOVE.

Love deals with all three roots simultaneously!

1 Corinthians 13:4-8 says that love is not proud or self-seeking, and 1 John 4:18 says that there is no fear in love.

So, the antidote to insecurity is LOVE.

Let's take the social setting where you don't know anyone. You feel insecure, but instead of being paralysed by a feeling, you decide to act. You decide to love. An action is more empowering than a feeling.

- You ask people about themselves.
- You offer to get them something to eat or drink.
- You notice who is alone or also looks out of place and reach out to them or include them in conversations.
- You pray that God will lead you to someone who you can encourage.
- You make an effort to remember people's

84

names. (Writing them down if necessary.)

You don't have to become the centre of attention, you just have to care about the people in the room. When you focus on loving people, what they think of you, becomes irrelevant.

3. Choose to be Content

As we said at the beginning of this chapter, the constant need for bigger and greater things can be an unexpected source of disappointment for an idealist. As invigorating as it is to strive to achieve or attain something, it can also be a major let-down.

contentment
/kənˈtɛntm(ə)nt/

a state of happiness and satisfaction.

What a great definition! Who wouldn't want to live in a state like that? As wonderful as it sounds, being content is difficult. A line from a Sheryl Crow song, sums it up well: "It's not having what you want, it's wanting what you've got."[66] We live in a world that is constantly telling us what we are missing out on, what we need, and what would make life perfect. That's a lot to take in, especially for idealists!

The Biblical standard for contentment is pretty radical:

We brought nothing into the world, and we can take nothing out of it. But if we have food and clothing, we will be content with that. 1 Timothy 6:7-8

---

[66] Soak up The Sun, Cheryl Crow. 2002.

While for people living in poverty, the idea of being content with having food and clothing may make sense; a wealthier audience may find it implausible. I think we might change the verse to say something like this:

We brought nothing into the world, and we can take nothing out of it. But if we have fine food and clothing, a nice home, a plasma TV, the latest iPhone, iPad (or the like) and a car...we will be content with that, for now.
First Me 6:7-8

Here's what we need to understand about contentment:

- It's not a personality trait or character strength that only some people have. It's a choice, a deliberate decision. King David put it like this:

  I have calmed and quieted myself,
  I am like a weaned child with its mother;
  like a weaned child I am content.[67]

- It is not based on what you have or don't have.
  Read Philippians 4: 11-13
- It is the realisation that you will not be better off, more capable or accepted, or satisfied with the thing you "can't be happy without."
- Finally, it is understanding that, in Christ, the secret to having it all, *is knowing that you already do.*

---

[67] Psalm 131:2

Jesus

There is no passion to be found
playing small – in settling for a
life that is less than the one
you are capable of living.
Nelson Mandela

A great deal has and could be written about Jesus... books, series, encyclopaedias, entire libraries! He is the best of the best. The perfect mix of every temperament, character, personality, and outlook. He encompasses everything. Mark was not exaggerating when he said this about Jesus:

People were overwhelmed with amazement.
"He has done everything well," they said. Mark 7:37

Although so much could be said about Jesus, we want to look at just three aspects of Jesus' character and teachings:
- His humility
- His ideals
- His help

1. The Humility of Jesus

humility
/hjʊˈmɪlɪti/

*the quality of having a modest
or low view of one's importance.*

This definition of humility seems difficult to reconcile with

Jesus. *A modest view of one's importance?* While we may easily be able to apply it to ourselves, how can it possibly apply to Jesus? There has never been or ever will be anyone *as* important as God's Son. The book of Colossians tells us that all things were created by Jesus, through Jesus and for Jesus. He made the universe (visible and invisible), and established every spiritual and physical law, from gravity and thermodynamics, to reaping and sowing. In him all things hold together. He is head of the Church, and through his blood he opened a way for men and women to be reconciled to God.[68] Jesus is supremely important. He is indispensably significant. Mankind's worth and hope are intrinsically pinned to him. So how can this definition apply to him?

While definitions are just man-made parameters to give meanings to words, we think this definition *is* an apt description of Jesus' humility. Here's why:

> The book of Philippians says that though Jesus was by nature God - he made himself nothing.[69] He chose to let go of his significance and his importance. He gave it all up, and became a vulnerable human being, limited by space, time and the physical laws that he had established. He chose to have 24 hours in his day, to feel tired and hungry, and to experience earthly sadness and loss. He chose to walk to places, to need sleep, food and companionship.

Jesus was humble not because of a lack of importance, but

---

[68] Colossians 1:15-17

[69] Philippians 2:6-7

because he chose to become unimportant! Why? So that we would have a chance to know our Father.

Perfect Submission

Even as Jesus submitted his importance, his rights and his will to God, he still understood personal desire. When we see him in the Garden of Gethsemane, we realise that he did not want to go to the cross. He really didn't want to suffer, but he wanted God's will more. God's painful, crushing will. We hear the conflict and submission in his words:

> "Now my soul is troubled, and what shall I say? 'Father, save me from this hour'? No, it was for this very reason I came to this hour. Father, glorify your name!" John 12:27-28

These words alone should be something idealists regularly pray! Idealists are masters at trying to avoid or manipulate their way out of suffering or difficulty. (Unfortunately to their own detriment.) But what an amazing example Jesus has set for us.

Even when God appointed Jesus as a high priest, Jesus did not feel entitled to it. The book of Hebrews says:

> Every high priest is selected from among the people and is appointed to represent the people in matters related to God … No one takes this honor on himself, but he receives it when called by God, just as Aaron was. **In the same way, Christ did not take on himself the glory of becoming a high priest.**[70]

Jesus deserved every title, position, and authority which God

---

[70] Hebrews 5:1-6

gave him as the resurrected Christ. But he never demanded it, insisted on it or took it upon himself. This is an essential quality, especially for idealists aspiring for leadership positions, to strive for.

Surely Jesus epitomised humility!

2. The Ideals of Jesus

ideal
/ʌɪˈdɪəl,ʌɪˈdiːəl/

a standard or principle to be aimed at.

When Jesus came to earth, he didn't change God's ideals or standard to suit the sorry state humanity was in. In fact he championed godly principles. He set them up as a beacon of light in the darkness. A place to anchor our souls. Because of how far gone the world is from God's standard, the ideals that Jesus taught can seem other-worldly, alien and unattainable. Some people have even called the Sermon on the Mount, "sentimental and impractical idealism."[71]

Did Jesus really mean it when he said:

Be perfect, therefore,
as your heavenly Father is perfect. Matthew 5:48

- Or what about his teachings on forgiveness, praying for our enemies, being blessed when we are insulted, handing over our cloaks and going the extra mile?

---

[71] www.religion-online.org/book-chapter/chapter-10-was-jesus-an-impractical-idealist/

- What could he have possibly meant when he said that *we* are the salt of the earth and the light of the world? And that the greatest in the Kingdom are the servants and those who become like children?
- Does Jesus really expect us to avoid lust and sexual sin at great physical cost? Are we meant to love God above our money, and not store up treasures?
- Are we genuinely meant to do to others as we would have them do to us?[72]
- Is it really God's standard that we must live as Jesus did?[73]

Absolutely! Which brings us to the need for Jesus' help.

3. The Help of Jesus

Jesus calls us to a heavenly standard. For an idealist, this can be a great source of inspiration and despair! This contradiction is brilliantly revealed in Peter's reaction to Jesus' interaction with the rich young ruler:

As Jesus started on his way, a man ran up to him and fell on his knees before him. "Good teacher," he asked, "what must I do to inherit eternal life?" "Why do you call me good?" Jesus answered. "No one is good—except God alone. You know the commandments: 'You shall not murder, you shall not commit adultery, you shall not steal, you shall not give false testimony, you shall not defraud, honour your father and mother.'" "Teacher," he declared, "all these I have kept since I was a boy." Jesus looked at him and loved him. "One thing you lack,"

---

[72] Sermon on the Mount Matthew 5-7

[73] 1 John 2:6

he said. "Go, sell everything you have and give to the poor, and you will have treasure in heaven. Then come, follow me." At this the man's face fell. He went away sad, because he had great wealth. Jesus looked around and said to his disciples, "How hard it is for the rich to enter the kingdom of God!" *The disciples were amazed at his words.* But Jesus said, "It is easier for a camel to go through the eye of a needle than for someone who is rich to enter the kingdom of God." The disciples were even more amazed, and said to each other, *"Who then can be saved?"* Jesus looked at them and said, "With man this is impossible, but not with God; all things are possible with God." Then Peter spoke up, "We have left everything to follow you!" Mark 10:17-28

How thrilling it must have been for Peter to witness this rich, religious young man fall at Jesus' feet, and "humbly" ask for the key to salvation. In love, Jesus laid down God's standard, but the young man walked away sad, unable to put God above all. The disciples were astonished. Not at the fact that the young man wasn't willing to yield, but at just how high God's standard was. They felt morally deficient standing in front of God's mirror. "Who then can be saved?" they asked one another. Peter finally spoke up, "We have left everything to follow you!" He had been enthralled by God's call and had given up everything to pursue it. Now he despaired that even that was not enough.

What is Impossible with Man, is Possible with God

Clearly the answer lies in Jesus response, "With man this is impossible, but with God, all things are possible." We cannot save ourselves, we need Jesus' help. God's standard gives us a glimpse into a life that could be. It is both exciting and challenging. Idealists can make the mistake of trying to live up to it by grit and sheer determination, believing that their passion will be enough to push them over the finish line. This will not only prove to be impossible, but a source of deep discouragement. We need Jesus to come alongside us and help us. (Or rather, we need to come alongside Jesus and follow his lead.) Jesus is well aware of our deficiencies. And he wants to help!

Therefore, since we have a great high priest who has ascended into heaven, Jesus the Son of God, let us hold firmly to the faith we profess. For we do not have a high priest who is unable to empathize with our weaknesses, but we have one who has been tempted in every way, just as we are—yet he did not sin. Let us then approach God's throne of grace with confidence, so that we may receive mercy and find grace to help us in our time of need. Hebrews 4:14-16

Jesus empathises with our weaknesses, he understands the temptations that surround us. He has been there. *He has been here.* He knows that we cannot do this on our own. Just as Jesus submitted to God, let us submit to him, approaching the throne of God's grace, and find the help we need to make it across the finish line.

On a Final Note

In *Healing of a Wounded Idealist,* we looked at Elijah and Peter as examples of wounded idealists who found their way back to faith. In this handbook, we have followed Moses' journey of growing humility, trust and faith. As we conclude we want to leave you with one last point to ponder.

In the book of Matthew it describes how before his crucifixion, Jesus took Peter, James and John up a high mountain, where he was supernaturally transfigured. The Bible goes on to tell us:

> Just then there appeared before them Moses and Elijah,
> talking with Jesus.[74]

Moses and Elijah arrived on the scene. Now, nothing in the Bible is coincidental or included without a purpose. So we have to ask ourselves, why did God choose these two men, of all the Bible heroes, to encourage his Son? Could it be that they would relate and know what to say to Jesus as he faced the greatest challenge of his life. It would be physical, emotional and spiritual torture. Jesus would face it all; the desire to avoid suffering, the potential disillusionment with God and his plan, the pain of rejection, the loneliness and the lack of appreciation. Moses and Elijah understood, and Peter (who God allowed to be there), would come to understand.

---

[74] Matthew 17:1

These men, whose stories could easily have blurred into obscurity, responded to God's call to obey despite their wounding and found healing along the way. Now *they were the ones chosen to encourage Jesus.* Surely God believes in and has great plans for idealists!

Idealist, God has a vision for you that is even greater than the vision you may have for yourself. Embrace the wounding, let it be the watershed that defines a new day of humility, faith and victory. God bless.

Appendix

The Guilt-ridden Idealist

Atelophobia
The fear of never
being good enough.

God has placed in each of us a conscience to help us identify when we have sinned or crossed a moral line. As Christians, we also have the Holy Spirit to further remind and teach us.[75] When we sin, our consciences are pricked, and we usually feel a sense of guilt affording us the opportunity to come to godly sorrow and repentance. Unfortunately Satan, who is the father of lies, has an unbelievable knack of distorting everything good, and can use this God-given mechanism against us. We can either be overly deceived, convinced that we are not "that bad," or overly accused, believing that we are the worst of sinners.

For the most part, the idealists we have spoken to, attest to having more of an accused personality type. If you are unfamiliar with the concept, a summarised description is given in the following chart:

---

[75] John 14:26

Accused Nature	Deceived Nature
Biblical example: Peter	Paul
Humbled through blessings. Luke 5:1-8	Humbled through difficulty. 2 Corinthians 12:7-10
Persistently feels guilty and accused.	Does not feel unnecessarily guilty.
Feels responsible for others' happiness and well-being.	Doesn't feel overly responsible for others' feelings.
Does not feel good enough.	Does not think they are *that* bad.
Blames themselves.	Can blame others.

If you are an accused idealist, our hope is that the thoughts we share here will be a help to find your way through the haze.

The Grace of God

The topic of God's grace can either evoke relief or dread in your heart depending on which way you look at it. For those who consider the grace of God an unattainable mystery, trying to understand it can leave you feeling defeated. You know intellectually that God's grace is good, you read about it in Scripture, and hear others speak about it with wonder-filled enthusiasm, but for you it holds discouragement. Another spiritual way of thinking that you fail at. Maybe you can relate?

If this is you, and you have been a Christian for any length of time, you may have resigned yourself to being motivated by guilt, duty and at times love and gratitude. But we believe that this is not as good as it gets and that *anyone,* including you, can get grace. The Bible teaches us that we can all learn to live by the grace of God and grow in our understanding of it.[76] It is not something that you either get or don't get.

Why It Matters

One of the teachers asked him, "Of all the commandments, which is the most important?" "The most important one," answered Jesus, "is this; love the Lord your God with all your heart, soul, mind and strength."[77]

This is the most important command we can obey in our lifetimes; everything else we do stems from obedience to this one command.

Love God with all your heart, soul, mind and strength.

Here's the deal, when we don't understand grace:
- We aren't able to love God with all our hearts, because our hearts are consumed by guilt.
- We can't love God with our souls because they are bound to the master of legalism and duty.
- We aren't able to love God with our minds because Satan's accusations dominate our thoughts.

---

[76] 2 Peter 3:18

[77] Mark 12:28-30

- And we can't love him with all our strength, because our energy is drained from processing life through the faulty belief that we are not worthy of God's love.

Without freeing ourselves from persistent guilt and duty, no matter how hard we try, we will always be held back from being able to love God fully.

Grace Defined

The dictionary defines grace as having God's free and unmerited favour. It is different from mercy or forgiveness. Mercy means to have compassion on someone or something and to offer them relief, and forgiveness means to cancel a debt owing.

Grace means we have God's favour. Imagine living every day believing you are favoured by God? Living, knowing that God doesn't just tolerate you but enjoys and likes you! For a deceived personality type that may be an easy concept to wrap your head around but for someone who lives with constant accusation, that can seem almost impossible.

The Jews, Our inspiration

The interesting thing is that God introduced the gospel of his grace, of his favour, during a time when the Jewish religion and society were peaking in legalistic "righteousness" and strict observance of the laws. The Pharisees and Sadducees walked the community as moral policemen making sure that all the rules were adhered to. Imagine for a moment being a Jew living under the Old Covenant and then Jesus arrives preaching a New Covenant of grace and favour. How difficult must it have been for a Jew to understand? They were being offered God's unmerited favour, apart from the 613 rules and laws[78] they had tried to obey their whole lives. They were being offered forgiveness of sins apart from the animal sacrifices they had known for generations… and you thought your background or upbringing was hindering your understanding of grace?!

The good news is, if the Jews can get it, we can get it. If God believed they would be able to grasp it, live by it and thrive (Acts 13:43), surely it is something we can understand as well.

Signs That You May Not Understand Grace

1. The first clear sign that you don't get grace is that you experience massive spiritual swings. One moment you feel like a spiritual superhero and the next you feel like an absolute wretch. What this exposes is your lack of understanding that we are never too good or too bad for God's favour. Nothing we can do can ever (ever, ever, ever) repay God for his salvation *or* cause him to no longer love you.

2. A second sign is constantly feeling guilty, not just when you sin but even when you are blessed. You feel overly guilty for missing an opportunity to do a good work, or for not being good enough, or productive enough or faithful enough.

3. A third sign is being "ok" with using guilt as a motivation to keep you on the straight and narrow. Sometimes we don't take our guilt seriously enough because we can see it

---

[78] www.jewfaq.org/613.htm

as a motivation. When we don't understand grace, we can fear that if we no longer feel guilty we may become flippant about our sin and fall off the path. What we don't realise is that our guilt is slowly eroding our relationship with God. The Bible teaches that it's the grace of God that should be our ultimate motivation. (Titus 2:11-14 ; Romans 12:1)

4. A fourth sign that you don't understand God's favour is that you try and use good works and "sacrifices" to try to appease or clear your conscience. Read Hebrews 9:9-14. The scripture teaches that as much as offering gifts and sacrifices were a part of worship under the Old Law, these acts were unable to clear the conscience of the worshipper. Living under the New Covenant, we can make the mistake of trying to appease our consciences with acts of righteousness. If it didn't work under the Old Covenant it will certainly not work in the New. In fact, in verse 14, it says that *only* the blood of Christ can clear our consciences. Nothing we can do (read, pray, fast, evangelise, helping the poor) will clear your conscience. Only the blood of Jesus has the power to do that. We need to take our guilty consciences to Jesus to clear them for us. Only then can we truly serve the living God!

THE BRIDGE OF HUMILITY

1. Go To the Dark Place

I waited patiently for the Lord;
he turned to me and heard my cry.
He lifted me out of the slimy pit,

out of the mud and mire;
he set my feet on a rock and
gave me a firm place to stand. Psalm 40:1-2

Satan lies to us, telling us that if we avoid our sin or sinful
temptations then we will feel worthy and maybe somehow
understand God's grace. But actually the opposite is true. It's
God's favour that gives us the courage to face our sin and hate
it, and not fear it.

When you feel yourself going on a guilt trip, rather than
running away and trying to avoid the feelings, take some time
to pray about what is making you feel guilty. We encourage
you to go to the dark places of your heart and acknowledge
your bitterness, impurity, hatred, pride, slander, self-
righteousness, anger, racism, prejudice, lust, selfishness,
rebellion, stubbornness, etc. None of us likes to go there,
especially not a guilty soul. We want to feel worthy. We want to
feel good and don't like seeing those parts of our hearts. But
this is the us that God sees, and this is also the us that is
covered by his blood.

Suggestion:
- Draw a diagram of a pit and then write in it all the sin (past
  and present) that God has rescued you from. Write down
  everything. This may take a while!
- The next step is to write down what sin you would have been
  involved in if God hadn't rescued you. We might not have
  done it all, but we certainly may have thought about it. We
  are capable of _all_ sin, given the right circumstances.
- If you have taken the time to really sit and think and pray
  through the above exercise you should be feeling humbled
  and sober about who you really are before God and how

desperately we need His mercy, forgiveness and grace.

If you are not feeling that, please take a little more time to go to the dark recesses of your heart and see what's there. It's not easy and takes plenty of courage to face ourselves in all our hideousness.

Now here's the amazing thing; despite all the darkness in our hearts, God still longs to have a relationship with us, and thinks that Jesus' death was worth it to save our souls! When Satan accuses you (and that is what his name means, accuser[79]), you no longer have to feel accused.[80] Because of God's favour, we are able to join Isaiah in saying:

Because the Sovereign Lord helps me, I will not be disgraced. Therefore I have set my face like flint, and I know I will not be put to shame. *He who vindicates me is near.*
Who then will bring charges against me?
Let us face each other! Who is my accuser?
Let him confront me! It is the Sovereign LORD who helps me. Who is he that will condemn me? Isaiah 50:7-9

When Satan whispers in your ear how worthless you are and the ways you have failed, you can say, "That's nothing Satan, I am way more sinful than that. *But he who vindicates me is near.*" We are able to live free from accusation. Yes, we are sinful, but we are covered in the blood of Jesus and that makes all the difference. We can live with a new confidence, knowing that we have God's favour. He knows every dark thing about us and yet He still treasures us! That is the grace of God!

---

[79] Zechariah 3:1

[80] Revelations 12:10

2. Remember

We came across a brilliant definition of grace:

Grace is when God gives us good things we don't deserve.
Mercy is when he spares us from the bad things we deserve.
Blessings are when he is generous with both.[81]

He gave me a firm place to stand.
> If we go back to Psalm 40, it says that not only did God lift us out of the pit but he gave us a firm place to stand. The truth is that if God hadn't rescued us, we would have wrecked our lives and others' lives as well. And yet instead of leaving us in our sorry state, he lifted us up and gave us a second chance. No one can go back and make a brand new start but by God's grace, we can have a brand new end!

Suggestion:
Take some time and write down all the blessings God has given you, (the Bible, prayer, Holy Spirit, friends, the church, family, health, a job, etc.) We deserved death and hell, but instead, God has showered us with blessings.

3. Combat Satan's Lies with God's Truth

Finally, fight Satan's lies with the sword of the Spirit. Below is an example of the verses to use to combat Satan's lies. We encourage you to write up your own list of the lies he's telling

---

[81] Unknown

you, and the scriptures you can memorise to combat them.[82]

Lie	Truth
"I'm not ___ enough for others to love me." (Good looking, smart, young, spiritual etc)	I am fearfully and wonderfully made Psalm 139:14
"If I told anyone about this area of my life they would reject me."	If we walk in the light, ... we have fellowship with one another and Jesus purifies us from all sin. 1 John 1:7
"It's my fault my _____ (husband, kids, parents) did _____ (some sin or action)."	The soul who sins is the one who will die. You will not share the guilt of another. Ezekiel 18:20
"Nobody understands me."	Jesus understands everything we have been tempted by, and all have sinned. Romans 3:23, Hebrews 2:17-18,
"I can't show any weakness. I have to be perfect."	My grace is sufficient for you for my power is made perfect in weakness. 2 Corinthians 12:9

Understanding God's grace and dealing with an accused personality type is a life-long journey, but we hope the few thoughts that we have shared in this chapter gives you a place to start. We highly recommend reading many other authors on the topic.

---

[82] Kim Pullen has written an excellent article that explains this further. www.disciplestoday.org/how-truth-frees-us-from-a-deceived-or-accused-mentality.

Recommended reading:
- What's so Amazing about Grace – Philip Yancey
- Transforming Grace – Jerry Bridges
- The Guilty Soul's Guide to Grace - Sam Laing

A Point on Perfectionism

Perfectionism is self-abuse
of the highest order.
A.W. Schaef

Being a wounded idealist puts you at risk of becoming a perfectionist. Perfectionism is an attempt to create the perfect world or at least an illusion of one. While it may be argued that perfectionism has strengths, the weaknesses far outweigh any good that can come from it. John Lennon once said in an interview that he was dissatisfied with every record the Beatles ever made, "There ain't one of them I wouldn't remake… including all my individual ones."[83] That's depressing, but perfectionism will do that to a person. It has the power to distort our view of reality and draw out any joy we get from living.

While striving for excellence is commendable, being a perfectionist can be a debilitating trap. Maria Shriver was so right when she noted:

> Perfectionism doesn't make you feel perfect;
> it makes you feel inadequate.

So how do you know if you have crossed the line from having high standards to being a perfectionist? For this, we turn to

---

[83] www.beatlesinterviews.org/db1980.jlpb.beatles.html

110

Celestine Chau's book, *How to Overcome Perfectionism.*[84]

Here are 8 signs that you may be a perfectionist.

1. There is **no room for mistakes and you can spot mistakes (real or imagined) that others don't see.** Whenever you see an error, you're the first to jump on it and correct it.
2. You have a **very specific manner in which things should be done.** You often find it hard to find the right people to work with; some may find it hard to work with you altogether. It's hard for you to get things done on time because they must be perfect.
3. You have an **all-or-nothing approach.** It's either you do everything well, or you don't do it at all.
4. It's **all about the end result.** You don't care what happens in between or what it takes to achieve the goal. You just want to ensure that the end result is attained. It's not uncommon for you to sacrifice your sleep, personal time, and well being, just to bring your work to the highest level.
5. You are **extremely hard on yourself.** Whenever something goes wrong, you get down on yourself.
6. You **become depressed when you don't achieve your goals.** You often mull over outcomes that don't turn out as you envisioned. You keep wondering "What if?" Most importantly, you feel that everything must be your fault if you don't achieve that perfect, desired standard.
7. **Success is never enough.** Whatever you do, or achieve,

[84] how-to-overcome-perfectionism-personal-excellence-ebook.pdf

you are not able to celebrate as there's always a greater height to aim for. Your life isn't very satisfying.

8. You **procrastinate just to do something at the "right" moment**. You are constantly waiting for the "right" moment to work on your goals. You only want to start when you are "ready," so as to deliver your best quality of work. However, this state of "readiness" never seems to come. Sometimes, it *never* comes as you perpetually wait just to get something done.

Maybe you can relate to one or more of these traits?

An Unexpected Trap

Being a Perfectionist is exhausting! It's exhausting for the perfectionist and it's exhausting for those who live with one. Brene Brown notes, "Many people think of perfectionism as striving to be your best. But it is not about self-improvement: it's about earning approval and acceptance."[85]

> I, Irene, have recognised that I want things to appear perfect as a way of avoiding criticism or judgment from others. But trying to maintain a perfect household, perfect appearance, and perfect behaviour from my kids can make me a crazy person. I have regularly joined the Pharisees in swallowing a camel and straining out a gnat;[86] pointing out the bad instead of praising the good. My poor husband has had to

---

[85] www.theepochtimes.com/interview-with-brene-brown-about-embracing-our-vulnerabilities_2339331.html

[86] Matthew 23:24

endure my constant "helpful noticing" of what could be better at home, with the kids and in church services. I have had to learn to hold my tongue and focus on what really matters *to God*.

The concept that, *mercy triumphs over judgment*,[87] is a difficult one for a perfectionist to get their minds around, but is one we must strive to understand. Although it requires a deliberate change of mindset and priority, we believe that as Christians, we can make strides in overcoming perfectionism.

The Spiritual Mind

As Christians, we are not immune to the deceptive illusion of perfectionism. The world has bought into its phoney allure and is constantly appealing to our worldly nature to do the same. Satan works to convince us that our imperfections make us failures and unworthy of grace. The spiritual remind rejects these accusations, and embraces (even delights in) weakness and imperfection because, if we let them, *they draw us to God*. The apostle Paul explained it like this,

"But he said to me, "My grace is sufficient for you, for my power is *made perfect in weakness*." Therefore I will boast all the more gladly about my weaknesses, so that Christ's power may rest on me. That is why, for Christ's sake, *I delight in weaknesses*, in insults, in hardships, in persecutions, in difficulties. For when I am weak, then I am strong."[88]

---

[87] James 2:13

[88] 2 Corinthians 12:7

True Perfection

There is only one perfect being in this universe, and we are not Him. God is perfect, his way is perfect (Psalm 18:30), his law is perfect (Psalm 19:7), and his will is perfect (Romans 12:2). Despite all this, God holds us to a standard of grace and not of perfection. He tells us to approach his throne of grace with confidence (Hebrews 4:16), so that we can find mercy in our time of need. He warns us against thinking that we are standing firm, but assures us that he is faithful and will provide a way out so that we can stand. (1 Corinthians 10:13) Perfectionism *is not* a way out. If anything, it is a way to guilt, shame and discouragement.

THE BRIDGE OF HUMILITY

- **Value relationship above productivity.**
  Martha was a perfectionist. She wanted everything to be perfect for her guests.[89] Jesus commended Mary for focusing on what mattered more, relationships. Relational connection is the most important thing on earth, firstly connection to God, then connection to others. Constant criticism and fault finding breaks or puts a strain on those connections. Don't underestimate the damage it can have long term on the health of those relationships.
  Ask those around you how much you encourage them vs. criticise and point out things?
  Take a month to decide that instead of trying to control everyone around you, you are going to love them.

---

[89] Luke 10:38-42

Before you give "helpful instructions," ask yourself if it's out of a desire to control based in fear or out of love. Don't give advice UNLESS someone actually asks for it. Bite your tongue.

- **Redefine failure.**

    We can never move forward if we are afraid to make mistakes. If there are past mistakes you have made, write down everything you have *learned* from those mistakes. Thank God for the lessons you have learned that you wouldn't have learned any other way. Don't let those failures define you, let them refine you, as it has been so aptly said, you learn more from failure than you do from success.

- **Embrace your weaknesses.**

    It seems like a paradox, but God can be glorified in our weaknesses. So often in striving to be strong we miss the fact that Jesus' greatest impact was not in the miracles, the fame, the sermons, or even in doing everything well,[90] but was in his weakest and most vulnerable moment, when he died on the cross.

- **Delegate and let go.**

    Let others help you. If you are a true perfectionist, that will sound sacrilegious, but God never intended for us to do all and be all. That is his job. We were created for community. Accept that it won't be perfect or done necessarily how you would like it done, but that's ok. In the grand scheme of things get some perspective.

---

[90] Mark 7:37

Take a deep breath and let it go. If God can handle and accept our imperfections, we must learn to do the same for others.

We hope that for all those striving for perfection, these things will help release your foot from a miserable snare and that you will find a safe place in your relationship with God.

The Insufferable province of Asia

*Courage is not the absence of despair,
it is rather the capacity to
move ahead in spite of despair.*
Rollo May

If you have been a Christian for any length of time, you will likely know the pain of when a friend or family member decides to no longer keep the faith. It can tear at your core, and for an idealist, it can feel intolerable. The Apostle Paul understood it all too well as he wrote his second letter to Timothy from a prison cell in Rome:

> You know that everyone in the province of Asia has deserted me, including Phygelus and Hermogenes. May the Lord show mercy to the household of Onesiphorus, because he often refreshed me and was not ashamed of my chains. 2 Timothy 1:15

How difficult must it have been for Paul to write these words, *everyone in the province of Asia had deserted him.* For modern readers without a full understanding of the context of the situation, it seems to come out of nowhere. Timothy obviously knew what was going on, but we can be left wondering.

What's up with the province of Asia?

While a realist may read these words and think, "It is what it is, even Jesus predicted that people would desert the gospel," for an idealist, this is one of those verses that can strike confusion, and even despair in their hearts.

There is a fair amount of debate among Biblical scholars as to what exactly Paul meant by this verse. They all agree that Paul was imprisoned in Rome at the time. Some believe that he is referring to his defence trial, which was not going well because those from the province of Asia failed to show up and provide testimony.[91] Others believe that Paul is referring to a mass apostasy[92] of the Asian churches,[93] which would be shocking if true. We personally think that the desertion he is describing is of those from the province of Asia who were supposed to come to his defence. (It is noticeable that he mentions Phygelus and Hermogenes by name, but doesn't call them heretics, as he does of Hymenaeus and Philetus in 2 Timothy 2:17.)

But We are Family

Either way, this was a very difficult time for Paul and would be for any disciple when trusted brothers or sisters decide to either no longer follow Christ or be a part of the church family. It is painful and can be deeply wounding, especially for idealists.

Having been disciples for decades now, we have experienced this wounding more times than we would like.
- Sometimes, it's a young Christian and it hurts to see them

---

[91] Liefeld, W. L. (1999). 1 and 2 Timothy, Titus (p. 237). Zondervan

[92] meaning: the renunciation of the faith

[93] Fee, G. D. (2011). 1 and 2 Timothy, Titus (p. 236). Baker Books.

return to something they desperately wanted to escape only a few months earlier. It is also difficult to foresee the pain they are choosing to bring back into their lives by selecting a path separate from God.

- Sometimes, it's someone who has become a friend over a few years. You have seen them persevere through trials only to now stumble at a trial that, to you, seems surmountable.

- But possibly the most painful is when it is a long-standing disciple, a trusted confidant, and dear friend who has been in the fight for as long as you can remember. Their lives and family are integrated into the fabric of the church. Their reasons for leaving are often very entangled and relationship complexities and hurts are almost always present.

But Why?

There are a few responses an idealist can have to this:

1. Something is wrong with me. "It's my fault, what could I have done differently? I feel like somehow I have let God and others down." This, in turn, depending on your coping mechanisms, can make you feel guilt-ridden or defensive and unapproachable. It may make you feel insecure in your walk with God.

2. Something is wrong with the church. "If the church was less structured or more structured, this wouldn't have happened," "if we were more youthful or less youthful," "if we focused more on the needs of the older disciples," "if we…" We can become overly critical of the church and the leadership.

3. This is unbearably disappointing. I will keep coming to church, but I am not going to invest as much time and energy into friendships that may or may not work out. I know the doctrine is right, so yes I may occasionally invite people to church, but it is not with the same faith, love and zeal as before.

Any of this ring true for you?

THE BRIDGE OF HUMILITY

People leaving the church family is a sad reality, but one that we need to make spiritual and emotional peace with. *We are not saying that we shouldn't care or let it be an excuse for poor shepherding practices*, but we must realise that even Jesus had many who no longer followed him.[94] In the Parable of the Sower, Jesus tells us that only one of the four soils makes it to the end.[95] He clearly understood the road to heaven is narrow and few find it.[96]

We have to have the humility to know that we will never do ministry better than Christ himself, or build churches more effectively than the Apostle Paul.[97] We must learn how to deal with losing friends in the faith, in a godly way.

---

[94] John 6:66

[95] Matthew 13:1-23

[96] Matthew 7:13-14

[97] We see it in the ministry of Paul, with multiple people abandoning the faith. See Galatians 1:6 and 2 Timothy 4:9-16 as just two examples.

1. Keep God's priorities straight

Jesus tells us that the greatest command is to love God above everything else and the second is to love our neighbour as ourselves.[98] We have noticed that people who *invert the two greatest commands* have the hardest time keeping a spiritual perspective on this topic. When people become more important than God, when church becomes more of a social club than a spiritual body, we have inverted these two commands. Our loyalty and love for God should always FAR exceed our love for anything or anyone else. Oswald Chambers said it like this:

> If I put my trust in human beings first, the end result will be my despair and hopelessness toward everyone. I will become bitter because I have insisted that people be what no person can ever be— absolutely perfect and right.[99]

Let's keep the two greatest commands in their correct order.

2. Guard your own heart.

Knowing how easily we can be led astray and lose our primary love for Christ should inspire us pay to attention to the words of Paul when he says that, "we should work out our salvation with fear and trembling,"[100] or as Proverbs tells us, "to guard our hearts above all else."[101]
Even Jesus warns that:

---

[98] Mark 12:28-31

[99] My Utmost for His Highest. Oswald Chambers. (1874-1917)

[100] Philippians 2:12

[101] Proverbs 4:23

> Because of the increase of wickedness,
> the love of most will grow cold.[102]

These verses alone should ensure that we are fully focused on keeping our own hearts in good shape spiritually. Let us guard against any forms of bitterness or criticalness, devoting ourselves *daily* to our walk with God and investing in vulnerable, spiritual relationships. Let us do this first and then strengthen those around us.[103]

3. Don't form umbilical cord relationships.

Research has shown that Christians who formed seven or more strong spiritual friendships showed a greater likelihood of persevering through trials than those that do not. Maybe that's why Paul encourages us to be devoted to one another in love[104] or why the Hebrews writer says we need daily encouragement so that we won't be hardened by sin's deceitfulness.[105]

We need multiple strong, spiritually edifying relationships in the church. Tying ourselves to one or two friendships makes it far more likely that we will be damaged by the defection of one of those friends.

---

[102] Matthew 24:12

[103] Luke 22:32

[104] Romans 12:10

[105] Hebrews 3:13

4. Treasure the fourth soil relationships.

But the seed falling on good soil refers to someone who hears
the word and understands it. This is the one who produces a
crop, yielding a hundred, sixty or thirty times what was sown.
Matthew 13:23

People with fourth soil hearts are rare and we need to treasure
them. You may ask, how do I know who they are? God knows
for certain, but we are given clues by watching them persevere
through trials and seeing how hard they fight to guard their
hearts. The continual growth in their characters, ongoing
repentance, spiritual influence and impact evidenced in the life
of non-Christians and Christians alike. Don't take these people
for granted. Treasure them, spend time with them. Have them
over into your home. Go away on holiday with them. They are
rare and should have a special place in our lives.

5.   Remember that God will not forget

The book of Hebrews gives us this encouragement:

God is not unjust; he will not forget your work and the love you
have shown him as you have helped his people and continue
to help them. Hebrews 6:10

Helping God's people is hard work, but God takes it as an act
of love towards him. He will not forget. He sees you and he
will reward you. Even Jesus had to remind himself of this truth.
In Isaiah 49:3-4, in describing the Servant of the Lord, it reads:

He said to me, "You are my servant, Israel, in whom I will
display my splendour." But I said, "I have laboured in vain; I

have spent my strength for nothing at all. Yet what is due me is in the Lord's hand, and my reward is with my God."

It can feel at times that our labour is in vain and for nothing at all, but it is at those times that we must remember that our reward lies with God. He is not unjust and will not forget the hours, days, months and years we have spent helping others.

In Conclusion

Paul begins his letter to Timothy telling him about the desertion, but he ends his letter with these words:

At my first defense, no one came to my support, but everyone deserted me. May it not be held against them. But the Lord stood at my side and gave me strength, so that through me the message might be fully proclaimed and all the Gentiles might hear it. And I was delivered from the lion's mouth. The Lord will rescue me from every evil attack and will bring me safely to his heavenly kingdom. To him be glory for ever and ever. Amen.
2 Timothy 4:16-18

What a man of incredible faith! Even though Paul experienced the pain of desertion, with some even shipwrecking[106] their faith, it did not cause Paul to shipwreck his faith. Our prayer is that the same can be said of us. That we will guard our hearts, looking to God as the anchor of our souls and our reward.

---

[106] 1 Timothy 1:19

A Comprehensive List of everything God and life owe us.

Nothing.[107]

---

[107] We deserve death and yet God has given us life. Rather than be entitled, be grateful for all the ways that God has blessed you.

Follow us on Facebook
www.facebook.com/helpfortheChristiancynic/

Made in the USA
Coppell, TX
04 December 2020

43084960R00080